My Life, My Faith, My Journey

Faith still moves mountains

Monica D. McGowan

authorHOUSE®

AuthorHouse™
1663 Liberty Drive
Bloomington, IN 47403
www.authorhouse.com
Phone: 1-800-839-8640

Published by AuthorHouse 4/10/2013

ISBN: 978-1-4817-1392-4 (sc)
ISBN: 978-1-4817-1391-7 (hc)
ISBN: 978-1-4817-1390-0 (e)

Library of Congress Control Number: 2013902649

FOREWORD
By Dr. Arthur Dawson, Jr.

To God be the glory! It is with an attitude of gratitude that I submit the foreword page of this book. A great deal of honor has been given unto me to have been chosen, especially knowing the author for a lifetime, watching her grow and being a source of help in the growth process by extending help to her family as a neighbor and pastor for many years. This precious woman walked through the valley and shadow of death at such a young age. God gave a word of prophecy through me to her mother concerning His purpose and the good that he would work through her after having gone through such an ordeal of a tragedy. God's purpose was to use her mightily as a pastor, teacher and leader in the work of ministry for the furtherance of the gospel and the winning of many souls to Christ, living a life as a humble spirited woman.

To be chosen as a writer and author, again, to God be the glory for the great things he is doing through her. Thank God for this blessed book titled: "My Life, My Faith and My Journey." I am fully convinced that this book will be a source of strength and encouragement as well as life changing for many of its readers. There are great lessons to be learned in life that may take us through different experiences as well as a process. We must have faith in God, who alone gives life and is able to form our lives to get us through every storm, hill or valley that life's journey may take us through. We must understand that our faith is our victory and without faith it is impossible to please God.

As we journey through life walking in faith, we can experience joy, achieve victory, obtain goals and finish well our course in life, holding fast to our faith without wavering. We can end our life's journey with confidence in a righteous God who will crown all who love his appearing. It is our life, our faith and our journey that should hold our focus until we see the King of Glory, never satisfied until we awake in His likeness.

Dr. Arthur Dawson, Jr.

Thank you!

To my parents: the late James Rauls Jr., Myrtle Rauls.

To my husband: Bernard, for the encouragement and the liberty to spread my wings and soar like an eagle.

To On Eagles' Wings Ministries: for your patience, prayers and continual support.

To my Children: Eris and Evan for the silence….lol

To God be the glory for the great things He has done and is doing in my Life, faith and journey.

It takes all of YOU to make this journey great.

My Life, My Faith, My Journey

Allow me to introduce myself, my name is Monica McGowan. I married Bernard McGowan in December of 1989. We have two adult children, Eris, who is now 23 and Evan, who will be 20 in March. I was born and raised in a small place in Georgia called Kingsland. I'm the youngest of eleven children. I grew up in a very large family with meager means. We didn't have a lot of material things but, we had love, and that made all the difference in the world.

My father worked as a long-distance truck driver, and that eighteen-wheeler kept him on the road. He loved that truck because it enabled him to take care of the family he had waiting for him back at home. I can still see him backing it in by the garage, which was across the street from our house, after coming off the road. My siblings and I would stand on the porch until he gave the signal it was safe to cross over. We would run over and jump into his arms. One of us in his arms, one would ride his back, and one of us would ride on his leg. It was always good when daddy came home, because his presence made the family complete. He often times brought gifts home for us. He would bring toys, clothes, shoes and souvenirs from places he had visited.

My mother was a stay-at-home mom. With 11 eleven children in the home, she too worked full-time. There wasn't time to do much for a family of this size but, go to church. We went to church and to school.

Mom was and still is, a Virtuous woman. A Christian lady with great Christian values. We went to church often, and when I say often, I'm talking Monday through Friday and all day on Sunday. Most Saturdays we would just enjoy playing outside with other children in our neighborhood, unless of course, there was something going on at church.

It would be in my grown up life that I learn the true value of having a solid foundation. My father's work ethics would teach me what to look for in a husband. It is my mother's spiritual values that would teach me not only how to be a mother but, more importantly how to be a wife. Just like my parents have laid a foundation for me to build upon, it is now my responsibility to teach my own children. In the end the only thing that really matters is what you believe and know to be truth. Truth which is founded on the Word of God will never change.

A peek into the life of others often offers insight that enables us to make better decisions. What to do in the face of adversity and strife is a decision best made before the situation arrives. When life backs you in a corner, who are you going to put your trust in? Every choice we make in life will bring victory or consequences. He came that we might have life and life more abundantly.

CHAPTER 1

My first recollection as a child was this beautiful white dress. An explosion happened in our community, about ten to fifteen miles from where we lived. And this beautiful white dress would be the dress I wore to my sisters' funeral. The explosion took place in '71, and I had to be around 4 years old. The local chemical plant that employed a lot of the locals exploded. In that explosion was my second-oldest sister, Sandra. My father had given us all nicknames, and she was called Runt. Daddy said it was too many of us for him to remember the names mom had given us, so he gave us character names. She was small in comparison to the other children, so he called her Runt. Runt was a part of the explosion, and our family would never be the same. Daddy was on the road during the time of the explosion but, returned as soon as he heard.

My oldest brother, James (Bubba), drove out to the plant to see if she was ok; along with half of the town's people. It was at the site of the explosion that he would ID her remains and then takes the long drive back home to tell the family. The family waiting and praying for a miracle would be informed that Runt was among those who had been killed.

The Thiokol explosion change Camden County forever. As a small child I did not feel of the sorrow of it per se, but what I do remember is that I wore this beautiful white dress. In my childish mind, I thought all the people that were coming by, came to see me in that dress. I had no idea they were coming to give my family condolences. It wasn't until I got older that I was made to realize the sorrow that particular memory was attached to.

The community lost many lives in that explosion. There were funerals going on daily for those who lost their lives in that awful explosion. Some that survive the explosion but was so severally wounded would past away days, weeks, months, even years later. Then there would be those who would never fully recover from their injuries or the memory of seeing bodies badly burned and dismembered lying all around them. At the age of 4, I don't recall the sadness or the horror and that would be impossible for a child but, thank God for the memory of that white dress. My sister Cheryl and I wore these beautiful white dresses, with white shoes and lacy white socks. We wore little white panties with the ruffles on the butt, and white ribbons in our hair. Being so young when the explosion happened, I was completely unaware of what really happened that day in Georgia, but I'll share with you what I learned as I got older.

I would hear my family and others in the community talk about the Thiokol explosion and the lives that were lost. To this very day, my family talks about the explosion and the daughter/sister/mother/friend that was lost. It's our way of keeping the memory of my sister alive. Whoever coined the phrase 'gone but, not forgotten' has proven to be correct.

When my sister died in that explosion she left behind a fourteen-month-old son. My mom would raise him as her own child until he was old enough to understand. In order for him to know of his mother, there had to be conversations that included her as often as possible in our home.

Rodney was raised in the house with us as a brother, and we referred to him as the twelfth child. It wasn't until we got older that that my parents would reveal to him and to the younger children that he was her grandson. The older siblings knew but no one ever said anything until mom gave the consent. God had taken a life but, He had also replaced the loss with this grandson. In every possible way, mom still had eleven children to raise. Rodney is a nephew by law but, a baby brother by love.

The financial benefits of my sister were given to my mother in care for her son. The benefit check wasn't much but, back in the day it made a huge difference in a house with eleven children. I remember my mother would buy diapers, clothes, soap, deodorant, and different things that were needed in the house.

My mom being a Christian would have days when she struggled with the loss of her daughter. She began to question her daughter's death at such a young age. She mourned silently for years. In one of our conversations, she shared with me her resolved. The Lord took one of her children so the others would not have to suffer as much. I believe her way of coming to a place of peace was accepting; as hard as it was, that God makes no mistakes. He's too wise to make a mistake and too just to do any wrong. And because we know; "that things work together for the good of them that loved the Lord, them that are called according to His purpose."

Situations in life will constantly test our faith. We must learn to pray for the answers even when the answers we find are hard to comprehend. It doesn't matter what others think or believe it only matters what we believe and hold as evidence to be true. There will always be those around us who will challenge every decision that we make. Our lives and times are in His hands. No one should be allowed to influence your life to the point that you begin living for them instead of yourself. Make a decision! Rather others agreed or not, know that it's your life. The good, bad and ugly that we travel through will make you into the person you were predestined to be. We will all have to give an account for every decision made in life. Even if it's wrong; it will work for our good if we have confidence in the Word.

CHAPTER 2

Religion is a huge part of my life. I believe in the Trinity. I believe in the Father, the Son, and the Holy Spirit. I believe the three are one. I serve as a pastor here in my community, and have done so for the last twelve years. I believe I was called into the work ministry at a young age but, I would have to journey through some rough places, in order to get the proper training. I know that where I am today is based on the truth of where I've journey and who was with me all the way.

I've watched my mother and the faith she has in God, and I'm happy to say "it has made all the difference in my life." My mother was really strong in her walk with God. She is remembered as a praying woman. Back when I was growing up in Georgia, we didn't have medical insurance as many of the other folks but, mother had a prayer life that's out of this world. I recall mother getting in a place of prayer and we would witness the supernatural power of healing taking place right in our home. The old saints would fast and pray until God came through for them. They literally took Him at His Word. I learned at an early age to put a demand on the Word. His word will not return to him void but, it will accomplish that in which it was sent.

Because there was no medical insurance, we hardly ever saw a doctor. The only way one of us went to the doctor, would have been because we were near death and I mean dying. For toothaches, earaches, headaches and all kinds of childhood sickness and diseases, Jesus was REALLY our doctor. Mother would work with the medicines she had available in the house. More often than not, we had Bayer aspirin and Noxzema in our medicine cabinet. One of the older children, who weren't sick, would have to walk to the downtown drug store to get these items, if she was out.

On one occasion I became quite ill. I had been in bed for a few days, maybe the flu, not really sure. My fever would not break and nothing mother did seem to be helping. Mother shut herself into the house, turned off the phone and the television and started praying. I recall her praying and talking to the Lord as she nursed me in that bed. When I could no longer eat nor drink, she began to plead "the blood." She came to a place where she felt I was not going to make it if she didn't get me to a doctor. But before she would take me to a doctor that she couldn't afford, she decided to take me to her pastor. She picked me up out of the bed, washes me off, and carried me to the house of the Lord. She places me on the backseat of the car, and she peacefully drives to the church as if all is well.

Once we are at the church, she parks the car and we sit and wait. The parking lot is empty and we are the only ones there. I remember the then pastor, the late, Elder T.J Myers. Elder Myer was a big, tall, older gentleman, with what seemed like, the biggest hands in the world. He would be the first to arrive for evening service. When he arrived to the church, he sees us parked out front. He goes through the back-side door and opens up the front door for us to come in. My mother carried me in, and he takes me from her arms. She begins to tell him concerning my illness as we walked toward the altar. I remember my mother saying, "I've prayed all I can but, I'm going to need your help. I need you Pastor to touch and agree with me."

By that time, another one of the ministers had arrived and is coming through the back-side door. When Elder Andrews came in and observed what was happening, he headed over to the altar to assist in praying. Pastor Myers dabs a little bit of blessed oil on my forehead. Elder Andrews places his hand on the shoulder of Pastor Myers. My mom stands with her hands prayerfully to her face as they all begin to pray. As they all begin praying, my attention is given to the voice of my mother. "I plead the blood! I plead the blood of Jesus" my mother said repeatedly. My mother stops praying and hurries over toward the kitchen area and return with towels. Just as I begin to throw-up, she places the towels under my mouth. The flem (mucus) that was resting in my body and holding an infection began to release itself. I wanted to but, could not stop it. It was as the Lord, himself had said "that's enough Satan, loss her and let her go." Elder Myers eyes assured me that everything was ok. I must have sat there throwing up for what seemed like hours. Pastor then looks in my concerned mother's face and declare "She's going to be fine."

I was helped up and laid on the pew next to my mom. Other church members had arrived and church service started. Somewhere between the service starting and the service ending; I was up and bouncing around, clapping my hands as if I hadn't been carried in just a short while ago. This was my first spiritual recollection and its one I will NEVER forget. I accept the fact that many may not believe but something happen for me that night in that little country church across the tracks. When we go to the scriptures, we will find the portion that says 'when sick, you should pray, call for the elders of the church and let them lay hands, and the sick shall recover' To me, that's been a powerful memory in my journey. When my mom couldn't get this sickness to pass, she took me, as the scriptures said, to the elders of the church, and they anointed me with oil, laid hands, and prayed the prayer of faith. I thank God for the doctors and the medical knowledge He's endowed them with, but my first decision will always be the prayer of faith.

This childhood event is a huge part of my spiritual journey. I said to people on many occasions that I once relied totally on the prayers and faith of my mother but not anymore. The Lord has proven Himself to me. This strong, supernatural influence is not make-believe or hocus-pocus. There is a higher power that works through us if we just have faith. I'm one who believes that if you have faith the size of a mustard seed, there are some mountains we can move. Faith simply put, is being assured in one's heart, that our heavenly Father loves us. I have a strong spiritual background and for that I must give credit to my mother and the church family at Georgia Avenue Church of God. I truly believe that the uncompromised Word of God is still able to move mountains. Thanks for embedding the Book into me. When I say the Book, I'm talking about the Bible.

The older Saints did not have the material possessions that our current generations have but, they had a confidence in the Word of God that demanded things happen when they came together in prayer. This type of faithful praying is absent in most of our churches today. New churches are being erected daily without the presence of an altar.

CHAPTER 3

Rauls is my maiden name. From what I understand, back in the day, black families' took on the last name of their slave owners. In order to shed some light on this journey, it is vital that we know our history. Our history tells us who we are, where we originated from and most importantly it reflects the progress we've individually and as a family unit. My Great-grandfather was Jim Rauls, from the big town of Meigs, Georgia. He was born a slave but, was able to do great exploits and leave a legacy for the generations that would come after him. I come from a lineage of strong, determined people. Even in slavery they were able to accomplish greatness and they did so while serving under the hand of harsh taskmasters. Before death, Jim Rauls was able to purchase his own land and leave it as an inheritance for his wife and children.

My grandfather was James Rauls. He was one of the three sons of Jim Rauls. He was lovingly referred to as "Big Man". Big Man left Meigs and came to Kingsland, Georgia, to find a better life. Why he ended up here, only God knows, but, this is where he laid his hat and settled down. He took to wife, Evalina Rauls, who originally came from Quincy, Florida. Now my Grandmother (Grannie), she was a businesswoman, and she came here because she had a lead on a business. My grandmother had one of the only black owned businesses in the community and she placed it on the busiest street in town, Lee Street, also known as Hwy

17. She had a (I don't know what to call it) a little jook-joint shop. She sold beer, alcohol, chips, pickles, pig feet, and kind of stuff. At night, she would turn on that old piccolo machine, and the people would kick up a dust, and dance for hours. We weren't allowed to go inside because the people would be drinking, and every now and then someone would want to fight. Grannie put the fighters outside but, if someone pulled out a knife or gun, she would pull out hers', and Grannies was always bigger. My siblings and I would seek over to the shop and seek through the back door. Everything would be fine until someone went and told my mother. My sister, Cheryl and I would dance for Grannies customers and they would give us a quarter or buy us chips and candy. This one time, Cheryl and I stayed too long and mother was walking in the door with a switch. Someone had gone and told her we were at Grannies shaking out butts and men were watching. She would beat us all the way home. Back in the day you couldn't run from your whipping and there were no such thing as calling 911 on your mom.

My grandfather, Big Man was the town's barber and men would come with their sons from miles all around. My grandparents were entrepreneurs and they were well respected in Kingsland as well as surrounding areas. Big Man and Grannie were able to purchase the front street property where their business was located and later they built two houses, one on each side of the business. Since then we've had to knock down her old house, and of course, the old shop but, the property still belongs to the Rauls family. My grandparents had 3 sons. My father, James and his two brothers, Uncle Clarence and Uncle Amos (Muke). Their three sons all stayed in Kingsland, got married and had huge families of their own. My father had eleven (plus Rodney), Uncle Clarence had nine, and Uncle Amos had seventeen. As you can see, their boys had lots of grandchildren for them.

Anyway, that's my daddy's history. He was a hard worker. He used to always tell us that he had kept the first quarter he ever made. When he passed away, we were able to go through some of his personal stuff, and sure enough, we found old money. Money that was older than we were that he had saved. He kept it in (what he called) a strong box that bared a little lock on the front of it. Daddy had a lot of history in that little strong box.

Chapter 4

When we get together for family gatherings, you'll begin to hear the talk about the history of the family. My grandfather wore a patch over his eye because he only had one eye, and he would scare the kids. When they got loud or bad, he would always uncover it to make them run away and get rid of them. Some of the older family members said he couldn't talk well, and he couldn't write. He never learned to read or write, so he used to mark an X on everything as his mark or signature. They said he would always say, "What you looking' at?" when people would stare at him after he lost his eye. The story is that he got in a fight and the other man pulled out a knife and Big Man got stabbed in the eye. I vaguely remember the black patch over his eye, but I don't ever remember him actually taking it off.

My grandmother used to always talk about sticking together when we got in fights. She told us that my sisters' fight is my fight. You couldn't come home and one person has been in a fight. When you got home, everybody better have a black eye. She meant that we were to stick together no matter what. She taught us that you don't let anybody mess with your family.

When someone would upset my grandmother or mess with someone in our family, she was always ready to go to war. Grannie was always saying she was going to kill everything big enough to die. When she passed, she had to have been a hundred plus years old. We don't really know; there wasn't a birth certificate to be found. In her day, slave births were written into the slave owners logged books. After times begin to change, those books were scattered and many blacks had no record of birth. My dad believed when we buried her she was 102 or 103, but still to this day we're not certain.

CHAPTER 5

Holidays were really special for my family. My dad always made the Fourth of July very special with a once a year trip to Little Tabot Island or one of the beaches in Florida. Easter was very special, as well. My sister, Cheryl and I always got new shoes and pretty dresses for Easter. After church we would change into our new ko-locks and head out to the Easter egg hunt back at the church. My dad worked hard while Mom stayed home with us, but he would always come home at the last minute with whatever mom had told him we needed. We grew up believing in Santa Clause and dad wouldn't have it any other way. We would fall asleep waiting up for Santa but, we were never able to see him. My father took really good care of his family. For the most part, we were better off than most people, when I look back.

By the time I turned 10 years old, dad was able to build a brand new brick home for the family. We left D Street and move out to Kinlaw. Today the house doesn't appear to be much but, back then we felt so blessed. Mom got a new car later that year and we thought we had arrived to the Promised Land. This house had hot running water and we would not have to boil water on the stove to bathe anymore. The roaches were left back at the old house for a while but, they eventually found out where we moved to and most of the faithful came and moved in.

We continued to go to church and school from our new location. As children of Christian parents, we were often teased by other children. Because of my mother's beliefs we were not allowed to wear pants or make up during our teenage years. We were jokingly referred to as the 'sanctified' kids. None of us had a clue as to what it meant. It would be much later when I discover the true meaning. I now know that we all have to been sanctified or set apart for the Master's use. I'm okay with it!

As teenagers growing up in the church we often went to revival. We wanted no one at school to know that we attend because we would be teased. We would often get saved during revival but, being saved at school was impossible. We always seemed to be outnumbered when compared to the children that did not attend church. We learned to get saved on Fridays, that way we would have all weekend to come together and plan how to deal with the kids at school. As far as I can remember, we remained outnumbered throughout those school years. But, each revival, we got saved again!

CHAPTER 6

When I graduated from high school, I couldn't wait to get out of my mother's house because going to church all the time was not optional. In her beliefs, we weren't allowed to do a lot. Especially her girls! We didn't go to football games, and we didn't date. There was a lot of stuff we just didn't do. In her mind and the minds of others like her, she was protecting us from what we were going to have to endure once we were older. We weren't allowed to do a lot of things, so when we all graduated, we immediately left home. We all wanted to be able to do whatever we wanted to do. In my case, I was the baby of the family, so I was a little selfish, I must admit. I left on graduation night and haven't been home to stay more than a few days since. As I prepared for graduation night, I also packed my bags. My oldest sister, Danette and I already made plans. Immediately after turning my tassel and saying farewell to a few classmates, I jumped into the car with her. Her graduation gift to me was a trip to Disney World down in Orlando, Florida. Once I got settled into her home in Jacksonville, I begin to look for a job. I got my first job at McDonalds and would stay there for a year before moving on.

My sister made sure I got to work every day. She taught me how to handle money and insist that I open a checking and savings account. I was given the responsibility of paying the water bill at her house. She gave it to me because it was the smallest of her bills and I insisted on helping since I was allowed to live in her beautiful home. Danette made things special. On the weekends we would go to the beach, club hopping, or hit the malls. She taught me the quality of a thing is far more important than the quantity. She allowed me to wear make-up only after she escorted me to a make-up professional in the mall. She insisted that too many ladies were wearing it wrong but, I was going to wear it right. I was allowed some eyeliner, mascara, lip-gloss or a light lipstick. She treated me like a young adult and the things mom wouldn't allow for the first time was allowed and I loved it.

My sister had a military spouse and he received orders for North Carolina. This meant they were moving and she and I both knew mom wasn't going to let me go that far out of her sight, no way, no how. Well we were right! So Danette moved to North Carolina, and I return back home to Georgia. I hated being back in Georgia and away from my sister. She had a way of making life seem so awesome and special. I had my things at mom's house but, I was living from house to house. I would stay a week with one sister, then a week with a brother, then to another sister's house. Mom had too many rules and once you get a taste of being grown and doing what you wanted, it's hard to go back.

Well, Danette got settled in Carolina and found a job immediately. After a short period of time she wanted me to come and live with her again. My niece Nicole, whom I lovingly call Smue, was in a strange place and she didn't want her to be alone. She was calling because she wanted me to come live with them in Carolina. Smue was around fourteen at the time and she didn't like leaving her home alone. She needed someone to take her to and from school and pick her up after band practice. I jumped at the chance to be with them again. Danette drove from North Carolina on Saturday morning and Saturday night she returned with me and my things in her car.

I left home. My mom didn't want me to leave home, but my sister was living in North Carolina, and I wanted to go be with her. Danette was everything I thought I wanted to be. Seeing her drive up in that smoke gray Porsche was the deal breaker. Just the thought that I would soon be behind the wheel of that baby sent reasoning out the window. My parents didn't want me to go, but I wanted to go just to get away. I just needed to get out of the clutches of their rules and government and get away from how they thought I should live my life. I was young, inexperience and green. I needed to do my own thing, and at the same time be able to help my sister. She had a daughter that she didn't like leaving home alone while she worked, so I went to live with her in Asheville, North Carolina.

I hadn't been in Asheville long, but I got settled in and decided I would find a job. I knew my purpose for being in Asheville was to help with my niece, so I needed something close to home with hours that would be convenient with Smue's schedule. My first job in Asheville was with Winn Dixie. The hours fluctuated so that I wasn't able to balance the time I needed, so I had to resign. The day I resigned happen to be on a day that I had decided to walk to work. We had a convenience store right there in the neighborhood that Smue and I frequently visited. As I walked toward home, I decided to stop in for a cold drink. As I approached the door, I notice a sign on the door asking for help. I filled out an application and was interview and hired the same day. Little did I know at the time, that this would be the place that my faith in a higher power would be put to the test? I started my new job as well as what would turn out to be a new ministry.

CHAPTER 7

This is where my faith takes the stand in the courtroom of life. My real purpose in writing is to give insight into the wonder working power of a loving God. Miracles are happening every day and I believe it's time to share mine with others in an attempt to inspire hope to someone who may otherwise feel hopeless. Since the time my mother carried me to the house of God for prayer until this very moment, I now know that He will never leave nor forsake me.

Train up a child in the way he should go and when he is old, he will not depart from it (Proverbs 22:6). In other words teach your child the way of the Word and whatever he get stuck in, that Word will swell up in him and prove to be life changing.

In 1987, on Halloween night, I was working at the convenience store. I had been on the job for a few months and things were going good for me. The schedule was what I needed and I didn't have to drive because it was right down from where I lived with my sister. It was a Friday night, and I had taken my niece and a few of her friends to a football game, when I got a call from a coworker who sounded awful. Her name was Sylvia, and she had caught the flu and couldn't go in to work. Sylvia worked the eleven-to-seven shift because it allowed her to be home to get her grandchildren off to school. She was an older woman and most often held down two jobs to make ends meet. She called and asked if

I would work her shift and she would owe me a favor. I knew that she would have worked it for me if I were sick, so I told her of course. It was our responsibility to find a replacement if we weren't able to be at work. After the football game was over, I took my niece and her friend's home. After dropping off Smue's friends, we headed for home. I knocked on my sister's bedroom door to let her know that I was headed to work because Sylvia was sick. I grabbed my name badge and my smock, locked the door behind me and begin my short walk to work. By this time of the evening, you had just a few trick-or-treaters out, but there were still a few ghosts and goblins running from house to house trying to get last minute candy before the porch lights were turned off.

Whenever I would have to work the late shift, I always drove to work. I never walked at night but the night was so beautiful that I decided to walk. My sister would have her husband drop the car off later once he got off from work. During the day, I would walk, because we were just a short distance away. I got to the store, and Carolyn, who was clocking out; begin to print her drawer receipts. After counting the money, she dropped it in the safe, and began telling me how busy the day had been. Trick-or-treaters had taken all of the candy the store made available for them. I clocked in, and she clocked out. Around eleven o'clock, everything seemed to slow down. My sister and husband came with the car. She would always grab a bag of chips or something whenever she came to the store. I made them stay a minute as I ran outside to turn the pumps off. She caution me for safety and they went back home.

I was alone in the store and hadn't had a customer in a while so I decided to go ahead and stock the freezer. The bell connected to the door allowed us to hear when a customer came in. I had been alone several times so this wasn't the first time but, it was my first Halloween night and I thought nothing of it. Anyway, there was a man who came to the store constantly. I couldn't stand him. He would make advances at me and he stank of cigarette smoke. He would rub my hand when paying for his merchandise and tell me how pretty he thought I was. He apparently thought I was very attractive, but, it got weird so I reported it to my supervisor. She told me not to encourage him in any kind of way, not to say anything, just to ring up his order. That was how we decided to handle it. She thought if I just ignored him, he would stop.

This particular night, he came into the store dressed as Dracula. I heard the bell and presented myself from the freezer to greet the customer. When I looked up, I saw a man in a Dracula costume. It was Halloween night, so that wasn't out of order, then I recognize it was him. I was always kind to the store customers, even him. I went and took my place behind the counter at the register. He then began explaining his costume. Apparently he had entertained some children at a local McDonald's for their annual Halloween party. He came in, walked over to the counter and asked for cigarettes. I knew his brand because he was a regular customer. I turned my back to get him the cigarettes, and then turned back around to lay them on the counter 'because I didn't want him touching my hand. I immediately notice he has laid a huge kitchen knife on the counter. When I looked up into his eyes, all I see is a void.

"Give me the money in the register." He says.

I didn't give him any feedback. I just opened the register, which didn't have any money in it because Carolyn had dropped the day receipts, and I hadn't had but one or two customers. There was all of maybe nine dollars in the register, but I gave him everything, including a marked two-dollar bill that stayed in the register. He asked that I put it in a bag, and I did. After he took the money, he grabbed me by the hand and put the knife to my neck.

"Now, come around here," he said, and he held my arm across the counter and walked me down to the end so that I could come around. He promised that if I do anything stupid he would stab me. I was to walk out the front door with him and get into his car.

He takes me from the store, and I get into the car from the driver's side with him holding my arm. He gets in, as he pushes me over and I'm made to lie down on the front seat with my head on his lap and the knife under my neck. He drives me to the next county, I believe, for what seemed like a million miles away, and into an empty field. Maybe this was an old crop field or unplowed land. He drives me down this little thin dirt road, way out into the midst of nowhere. All I can see is blackness. I can't see any light in any direction. There are no streetlights or road signs. On this particular night the only light that can be seen is coming from the moon. The miracle God was about to perform would be done by heavens light. He drives to a particular place, and the car suddenly comes to a stop.

"Sit up and take off your clothes." He demands.

I sit up, and I take off my clothes. At this point, I know he has a plan and it's not in my favor. I try my best not to anger him but, I can't figure this thing out. Lord what I wouldn't do to be back in Georgia, in my mother's house. All of a sudden, mother's house looks like a palace. How I long to be under the safety of my father's roof. We both get out on the driver's side, and we both get into the backseat. All the time he has this death grip on my arm and a knife snuffed into my side. Once in the back of the car, he demands oral sex. This is something, I've never seen or done but from the direction he pulls my head, I respond. I realize I am in great trouble, and I do my best not to aggravate or anger him. I just kind of do whatever it is that he wants me to do. I loved my daddy! I do but, for some reason, I never told him. Lord, please give me the opportunity to let daddy know. I need to tell him that I appreciate him for taking care of me. I need to let my nephew, Dana, know how much he means to me. All the people that I loved but, never told consumed my thoughts as I feared what he was going to do next. If my dad was here, he would take care of this for me. If my brothers were here, they too would protect me from this animal. My mind raced with all kind of thoughts. My sisters would even step in and attack this person who's attacking me. After all, Grannie had taught us to fight together. After he had done everything to me that he could do sexually, he says to me, "Put your clothes on."

I rush to put on my skirt and my smock, but I don't put on any shoes. I don't have my shirt, bra, or panties and I don't bother searching for them in the dark. At this point, I'm praying he'd let me go as I promised to tell no one. With a prideful tone, he tells me this is not his first time doing this. We both get out of the car with him still holding me by the arm. I'm made to get out first, as he continues holding me by the arm. He then says "I've raped and killed 3 other women. Once we are out of the car, he begins his assault. With blunt force, he begins stabbing and slicing my body his knife. I turned around and grab the hand that he had the knife in, in an attempt to stop him and he nearly cuts off my right thumb. My right thumb is severed, and I'm looking at it, as it barely hangs on to the rest of my body. I take my left hand in an attempt to secure my severed thumb.

I instinctively recall the knife circling around my neck. A circling like he was attempting to cut my head off. Immediately the thought of my dad cleaning the deer's and hogs he would hunt, appeared in my mind. As a little girl, we would sit in the house and watch out the glass door as he gutted his kill every winter. I thought this is what that feels like. To this day, I unable cut up any meats in preparation for family dinners. This man was literally trying to cut my neck off. In the struggle with the knife, I am stabbed in my head, and I am stabbed in the back. This is way too much for me and I simply stop struggling with him. He's much stronger and I was only making it worst.

In that moment, I'm thinking, *I want to be dead. Lord, just let me die, I prayed. I'd rather be dead than this; I can't take this.* I run out of strength and collapse.

I vaguely remember him dragging me, I guess away from the car. He then covers me up with bushes and debris. I then see the taillights of his car as he drives away. He drives off with complete confidence that I'm dead. Now, to me he was a quiet man. He wasn't cussing, and he wasn't doing a whole bunch of stuff you would think somebody would be doing in that moment. He was just trying to get the job done, I guess, that he had preconceived in his mind and then get back home.

I am covered up and left for dead, and he is gone. I wanted to be dead, but I couldn't die. I couldn't die because I believe God had a plan and a purpose for my life. Anytime there is a plan and a purpose for your life, the enemy can't do anything to you until that thing comes to pass.

I remember lying there, thinking, *oh my God, I have six brothers. If they were here, they could help me. I've got five sisters. If they were here, they could help me. Oh, if only my dad was here...*

And I remember thinking, *I love my daddy, but he'll never get to hear me say it. Oh Lord, if I could have another chance...*

All sort of things are running rapid through my mind. I remember a voice speaking to me, though there was nobody there but me. It was almost if the Lord himself was saying *I'm all you got; what are you going to do? Your dad, brothers, nor your sisters can help you. I found out in that moment that you'll never know God is all you need until He's all you've got.*

Growing up, we went to church all the time, Monday through Friday, and all day Sunday. We had a Tuesday night YPE, which was the Young People Educational Bible night. In those YPE trainings, they taught us Psalms 23, Psalms 1, and Psalms 121. We learned to recite those verses of scripture until they were embedded in us. I remember laying there between life and death with my thumb severed and the light from the moon beaming down on me. *I could feel the warm blood running down my body but, I wasn't sure where it was coming from, felt like everywhere. There was so much blood! Surely I can't still be alive with all this blood running from my body. Maybe I'm dead!* Then out of the depts. of my soul comes "The Lord is my Shepherd; I shall not want. He maketh me to lie down in green pastures: he leadeth me beside the still waters. He restoreth my soul: he leadeth me in the path of righteousness for his names' sake. Yea, though I walk through the valley of the shadow of death, I will fear no evil: for thou art with me. Thy rod and thy staff they comfort me. Thou prepare a table before me in the presence of mine enemies: thou anointest my head with oil; my cup runneth over. Surely goodness and mercy shall follow me all the days of my life: and I will dwell in the house of the Lord forever. I began to quote the Twenty-Third Psalm over and over. A peace that surpasses understanding consumed my being and I knew that I was in His presence. I couldn't see a face but his voice and his presence is unlike anything in the universe.

I knew I was in trouble, at the same time, I knew time was not on my side because blood is literally flowing from my body. In my state of panic I began to move in the direction of the voice that had taken control. Something compelled me to get up. I remember thinking I didn't want to get up and I don't have the strength. There was a force that picked me up and caused me to stand erect. The bushes that once covered my body fell off me and back to the ground. As, I peered into the darkness of the night, I was made to see a speck of light.

In the midst of wanting to be dead, there was something so supernatural that happened—a light in the mist of all the darkness shone and it was to lead me to a place of safety. I'm standing there, wanting to be dead, but in the same breath wanting to live. I see this light, as I debate within myself. Maybe, I'm hallucinating; this can't be real, can it? In this conversation, I'm commanded to get up, so I get up, and somehow I begin to make my way toward the light far off in the distance. As I get closer to the light, it appears to be a small house. I make my way onto the porch and bang on the front door. I'm standing on this front porch when this elderly white lady peaks through the curtains. Now, I'm half naked, and covered in blood. I can only imagine what went through her mind seeing me standing there on Halloween night. She shuts back the curtains and turn off the porch light. I slide to the floor and begin begging for help. "Madam, I'm a good girl, my mom raised me in the church. My phone number is 904-555-5555, and my address is 1234 Any Lane, Asheville.

I begged and pleaded for a while, to no avail. At one point, I just wanted a drink of water. "Ma'am, I'm not a bad person. Please help me, please help me." I'm lying on the porch, bleeding everywhere and thinking to myself, I'm not moving, if I die, it's going to have to be right here because I'm out of strength for real

Through the darkness I can see the curtains move as she tries to pin point my exact location on the porch. Can I please have a drink of water, I plead once again. A man's voice respond, which I will find out later, was her husband and says, "Miss, we can't give you any water, you've lost too much blood. We've called for help and their sending somebody now."

I would come to know later that they turned off the porch light because they were afraid that whoever attacked me, may have still been in pursuit of me. And turning off the light would help protect me if so. I got help from the little man and woman that lived way out there in the country. They had called the police for me and they finally showed up. Because of them, I was able to get help. I'm alive today because of the call that was made by them for me and for that, I will forever be thankful.

Now, my assailant was a white. I'm lying on their porch, and this car comes up, and these two white guys get out. It was the sheriff and one of his deputies, but when I see them, all I see is white men. After just having been attacked by a white man, I found the strength and began to fight. The rural area that I had been taken to was far out, in the middle of nowhere. The road was so narrow that the ambulance couldn't drive down it. So, the officers had to come to the house and drive me to the road where the ambulance was waiting.

This one officer, a really big guy, picks me up and bear-hugs me, "Ma'am, we're trying to help you" he yells. He grabs me, and we get in the backseat as he pleads, "Please stop fighting; we're trying to help you." The other guy, of course, is driving the car.

We get up to the end of the road, and there's an ambulance waiting. I remember being in the ambulance but not getting out of the car. A young female paramedic with long pretty hair looks down at me as I lay in the ambulance bed. When she looks at me, her eyes bring such peace and I stop fighting and relax. I remember distinctively and will never forget her words. "I don't know who you are, but God's got an angel watching over you." I calmed down, as much as possible, and felt safe. I felt like I could finally rest. For some reason, I felt safe with her. I placed, what was left of my life into her hands and fell asleep. Two strangers, who would never see each other, again, had somehow established trust.

CHAPTER 8

I remember making it to the hospital. I was cold and trembling. I remember someone placing hot blankets on me in an attempt to warm me. I'd lost a lot of blood and my temperature had dropped tremendously low. After that I'm kind of in and out of consciousness. My next memory of this night is me on a gurney, being pushed down a white hallway with a black line down the center. I recall lying on the gurney saying, "Oh God, I didn't make it. I never told my dad that I love him." Please tell him, he was the best dad and I'll always love him.

Then, all of a sudden, I see lights and heard cheering. My family members had driven from Georgia along with many of the locals who had learned of my disappearance. They were all cheering and clapping and I knew for certainty that I had somehow survived. Strangers along with my family were waiting with flowers and gifts in hand. The local news reporters were there with cameras and note pads, waiting to update the community on my condition. I had been in surgery, I would find out later, for over eight hours.

There were specialists called in to put me back together. The nerves and muscles in my thumb had been severed and doctors were being extremely careful. The stab to my head had penetrated my scull but the damage was minimal due to the hardness of the scull. The stab in my back had punctured my lung, which made breathing difficult for a period of time. The doctors explain that the juggler vein in my neck was missed by just millimeters. I would have died almost instantly because I would have bled out. At this point, I'm trying to take it all in when my mother breaks the line and rushes over to my bed. "He touched your flesh, not your Spirit" were here exact words. I remembered how beautiful mother looked that day. And as she looked at me, all she saw was her child, her baby girl.

The police were there, and had been all night. Apparently someone stopped into the store and when no one responds to the call for service, they called the police. The cops came, my sister was called and the store manager. They begin to try and put the pieces together and they all dread something bad had happen. My sister knew I'd never go anywhere without letting her know. My car was parked outside, the register was empty, and the door was left unlocked. My sister had to call my parents in Georgia and give the awful news, that I was missing and it didn't look good. .

My mother looks at me and says, "Monica, he touched your flesh, but he didn't touch your spirit." Isn't that powerful? I tell people the doctors performed the medical surgery, but my mother did the spiritual and mental surgery.

They put me in a private room, and allowed my family members to come visit me one at a time. Now my mother wasn't moving from my side. Mother stood by my bed and she wasn't going anywhere. I knew I looked hideous because of the look on my brothers' and sisters' faces, but understand, my mom is standing there looking at me like I looked beautiful. The reason I knew I was hideous was because everyone that came in the door couldn't even come all the way to my bed. My brothers, sisters, aunties, and uncles, would make two steps in my room, see me, and turn completely around and head out the door. A couple of them began to throw up. Some of them passed out. They couldn't even come in the door. But I'm looking at my mom, and she's just standing there looking at me like all is well, I am beautiful. But I was wrapped up, and I was banged up, and swollen, I was a horrendous sight to see.

At that point, I don't recall exactly how I felt. We were all of adult age during this time. I was around nineteen at that time, so my brothers were about thirty. I remember thinking to myself, *these are grown men. I must look horrible, but I am so happy to be alive. Y'all just don't know—I get another chance to tell you I love you.* My dad couldn't come in the room because he was so upset. He was angry at the world because this happened to his baby. My mom just stood there, rubbing my head. My head was covered with bandages because I had been stabbed in the head. Her demeanor was that all was well. I remember thinking, *Okay, Mom, if everything is fine, and then what's wrong with them?*

The doctors allowed me to rest before the police were given permission to interview me. My mom prompted me for what was about to happen so that I wouldn't be overwhelmed. Two female officers entered my room and began telling me about the ongoing investigation and what they had found out. All of my co-workers had been questioned and it was discovered that my assailant had stopped by the store wearing his costume on his way to the Halloween party. He gave them the same info that he had given me. The officers stated that they had gone to McDonald's and got his name and address. They had him in custody but, I had to identify him.

I'm then handed this very thick photo album. My mom takes and lays it on my lap and she begins to slowly turn the pages. My heart is racing. I really don't want to ever see him again. I feel a little relax when we come to the half-way mark of this photo album, because I'm thinking he's not in here and I don't ever need to see him. My mom flips and the very next page, right near the top, I see him. I begin to weep uncontrollably. Mom closes the album! Silence falls over the room. One of the female officers steps over to my bed, "Monica, you have to put your finger on him for me, honey." Honey, she says, with the photo album in her hand, we can't charge him, if you don't point him out". Mom opens the book to where it was when I lost it, and there he was staring at me with those void eyes. My right hand is in a cask and in a raised up positions, my left hand is also swollen with stitches to the top and above the wrist. My mother takes and helps me place my hand on the albums page and then is made to stand back by the officers. At this point there's not a dry eye in the room. I looked down at my hand with all the stitches and I place it directly on his picture. "Is that him", is that the man that attacked you". I turn my head away from the photo, with my hand still on the picture, "yes, that's him".

The officer picks up her radio and says "that's him, we got him".

This is the part of my journey that truly prompted me to write my story. So many people go through horrendous situations like mine, and they never find the inner strength to keep living. The Word declares "that all things work together for the good of them that love the Lord, them which are called, according to His purpose (Romans 8). The ugly things that I've had to go through in life have somehow made me a better person. It was for my good but, God gets the glory. When we look at life through the Word, things look different. His thoughts are not our thoughts; His ways are not our ways. Every day is a gift. We have to choose to be happy or sad. Why continue to be a victim when you've made it out of some horrible ordeal. You are no longer the victim, you're the victor. It happens but, we made it.

So many walk through life with wounds that seem, they will never heal. I offer to you, myself as a living testimony. Only God can heal a wounded soul. Many, including myself turn to alcohol, drugs, relationships, food etc. in an effort to subdue the pain and like myself, find those things only make matters worse. We have to face our dark places or they'll take over our lives.

After my ordeal was over, I began to see a psychiatrist. I had not returned to my old self and my family became concerned. I kept to myself and became gravely depressed. I had been abducted. The scars on my neck were visible and I had to deal with the fact that I'd been raped. I was happy to be alive but, not like this. Every day I seemed to struggle with the shame of what had happen. I felt as if everyone was looking at me, as if I was dirty. I couldn't become small enough to go un-notice and truly that's all I longed for.

The first psychiatrist that I visited was a white male. We had no idea when the appointment was made that the doctor was a white, male. Neither did anyone predict my behavior when left alone with him. When the receptionist led me to his office and closed the door, I panic. All I saw was a dangerous white man. I had somehow put all white men into one category and none could be trusted. My sister was called back into the office to calm me down. She and the doctor both agreed that a female would be better for my case.

After this ordeal, I really didn't want to go back. Being out in the public was hard for me and to top it off, now I'm seeing a shrink. Not only am I ugly, I'm crazy too. I felt so alone, like nobody understood me. I went through a series of doctors until I finally found one that I was comfortable with. One of the doctors predicted that I would never be normal. I'd never get married and have kids. When my mother heard this, I never returned. Mother declared that only God has the authority to predict my future. And once again, mother was right. I'm living a pretty normal life. I'm married and I have two grown children. As a matter of fact my husband and I have been together twenty-five years. We both have college degrees and both our children are college students.

Never allow one persons' opinion of you to be finite. I often wonder how much different my life would be if my mother hadn't been there to intercept the negative words spoken over me during this vulnerable time in my life. Life and death are in the power of the tongue. Words have the power to build up as well as destroy. My mother spoke life over me when I didn't have the faith to speak over myself. Today, I speak life over myself as well as others. I'm able to minister effectively to other men and women who have gone through similar situations. I'm here to let them know that they don't have to remain the victim. There is life altering power on the inside of you. We must learn to speak over our own selves and stop waiting for someone else too.

CHAPTER 9

After my recovery the trial begin to take shape. I would return to Georgia only after the courts had rule on my case. My mother and father attended the two day court hearing with me. The attorney briefed us as to what would happen, and my possibly having to take the stand. My father seemed a little anxious the first day of the trial as was I. For the first time since that awful night, I would see the face of my attacker. My stomach was in knots and I haven't eaten anything. We entered the courtroom first with my attorney. I remember the smell and the coldness of the room. I really didn't want to be there but, I had no choice. This man tried to kill me and I must point him out. As we all sat there in thunderous silence, my attacker and his attorney enters the room. The frail women following them would turn out to be his mother. She had come to support her son and testify on his behalf. I immediately recognize him and turn my face in the opposite direction. When my body shifted, my father knew instantly that this was my attacker.

Dad stands to his feet with his hands in his pocket and says "Your Honor, please, just give me 5 minutes with him". Mother stands, takes dad by the arm in an attempt to restrain him and he pulls away. My attorney stands and turn to face my father, "Mr. Rauls, I need you to please sit down" he says forcefully. Dad begins walking toward my attacker and his attorney. My attorney braces himself in front of daddy and prevented any more forward movement. At that point the Judge asked my father to sit down and remain silent or he would have him escorted outside the courtroom. Well, dad didn't take his seat and he didn't shut-up. The fury in him was like nothing I've ever seen. Dad wanted to kill this man. He was escorted out by two armed officers and wasn't allowed back into the proceedings. Daddy was deemed a threat and was made to stay in the hallway both days of the trial. Mother and I would find out later that daddy brought a knife and a gun. Daddy came to kill the man that hurt his daughter.

After the charge was given and my attacker stood up and plead not guilty. My attorney turns to me and informs me that I will have to take the stand. He apologizes but, we knew it was a possibility. I move like a snail toward the stand. I'm sworn in then take a seat. My attorney begins questioning me about the night in question and I begin to weep uncontrollably as I relive that night. We stop several times in order for me to pull myself together. When I finish giving my recount, my attorney walks back over to me and asks the question "Is the man that attacks you in this room?" I respond "Yes". He then asks "Will you point to that man for the court?" I hadn't looked at him the whole time I was giving my testimony but something came over me and I stood to my feet and point directly at him. My attacker turns his head downward. He refused to look back at me. For a moment I felt sorry for him. He looked ashamed, wounded and lost. Like a small child.

"She provoked him, a small feeble voice declares, she provoked him. My son would never do anything like that. She's a liar." She then sits back down with face in hand, weeping pathetically. It was his mother. Apparently her husband had passed and he lived with her. He was their only child and like most mothers', she didn't raise him like that. My mother looks over at his mother weeping and could be heard saying "Lord have mercy on this mother." My mother believes and I do now that I have my own children, that there is no love like the love a mother has for her children. This woman was widowed and now her son is headed to prison for the rest of his life. In the mist of life crisis, don't forget that you are not the only one hurting. My mother is a beautiful spirit and has been since I can remember. She tends to look to the well-being of others in any given situation.

After two days, the trial came to an end. My attacker was given 3 life sentences without the possibility of parole. And I was given the honor of knowing he would never do this again to another woman. I walked out of that courtroom that day knowing that I'd done what was right and necessary.

When trial was over, my parents insist I return home with them. In coming back to Kingsland, I began to drink a lot. I didn't know how to deal with what had happened to me. I still felt ugly. Understand, I have visible scars on my neck; he tried to cut my head off. I've got these scars, and they're all over me. My arm was in a sling for a long time because they had to reconnect the nerves and veins in my thumb, which had been severed. So, I walked around with a hand piece on my hand and scars on my neck and my head. I just felt ugly, so I began to self- medicate with alcohol. I stayed to myself most often and would do nothing but drink. We had a little bar in town that is closed now, but I would sit there, and sip on Hennessey and Coke all day. When I was good and drunk, I would drive myself home. I stumbled to bed only to get up the next day and repeat the cycle.

One day while sitting in a drunken stupor at the bar, my cousin Jerri came in. I was drunk but, I heard her say "Lord, send somebody to see about Monica." Most of the locals who frequent the club knew me. I came so often that I would back my red car up to the front door. Before getting wasted, I would often help the owners, stock shelves or take out the trash. I was the first customer and on a few occasion the last customer.

On Sundays, I would go to the beach after church. I always went to church regardless of how lost I was in life. That is one of many things mother had instilled in her children. The foundation had been laid and no situation yet has proven to void it. On this particular Sunday while at the beach my brother-nephew Rodney, that my mom raised, would be there. He was there with a few friends. One of whom would be Bernard and he and I would later marry. I didn't know Rodney's friends, but come to find out we were all from Camden. They were all on our high school football team. I never knew Bernard while in school. After we begin dating, he would pull out our high school year book to prove his existed before this day at the beach.

Anyway, on this particular Sunday at the beach, they had driven over to take a challenge. You know how young boys are at eighteen and nineteen they were there to fight. The guys from Camden County were fighting some guys from Nassau County. The Nassau guys felt like Camden guys were coming to take their girls. A group of our boys began fighting a group of their boys. Bernard had gotten hit in the face with something; and had a massive whelp on the right side.

I am sitting in my car, drinking like I usually did, with the music on. Bernard comes and get in my car with me. He just opened up the door, got in and said, "Drive." I'm thinking *who are you?*

"Drive off," my nephew said, as he came to my side of the car, "Take him some place to cool down."

"I don't' know him" I replied.

"I know him and He's cool, this is Tex" he says to me with a sense of urgency.

I cranked up the car, and drove off. That's how I met my husband: on the beach, drunk, and he had just gotten in a fight. We drove to a nearby restaurant where we sat and talked for hours. I was trying to figure out who he was and what was going on. Later on, we returned to the beach. Once the sun went down, the clubs would open and I loved to dance.

My brother, Scooter (we called him) was the DJ and I always got in for free. I just needed to find out which club he would be spinning records in and let him know I was coming.

At about eight o'clock, the club opened, and my brother began to spin records. Bernard and I went inside, and of course, I kept drinking. Bernard sat at the table, and I kept drinking and dancing. At some point Bernard felt like I had gotten too drunk to drive myself home. He gives my brother, the keys his car, and he drives me in my car. After that, much is vague. I wake up in this tiny bed. It had to belong to a child. Bernard is sitting across the room watching me, as I struggle waking from my hangover. *"Who are you? And where am I?* He fills me in on the night we had and toss me my car keys. I knew he had to drive because I have no ideal whose house I'm in. I feel for my clothes and they're all there. He must be some kind of weirdo. Most men would take advantage of this situation.

After that, we would get together for dinner. Most often I paid for myself and he paid for himself. I wasn't looking for a boyfriend and that was my way of letting him know. We went half on everything and I mean everything. I drank a lot and Bernard began to notice and didn't like it at all. I was drinking because of my accident and had been for a while. It was my way of dealing with my abduction, but he didn't see it that way. He says, "It seems like you have to drink to be with me," The first couple of times he says this, I just stare off into the distance in silence. I was trying to understand what the man was trying to say. I've never had to deal with the emotions of another person so I really didn't know what to say. I knew he hadn't caused me to drink. As a matter of fact since I meet him, I haven't been drinking nearly as much as I was.

One night after we had checked into a hotel, I broke open my bottle as usual and he says it again. "Monica, do you have to drink just to be with me". I look at him and emotionally respond," I don't drink to be with you, I drink to be with me. Don't you remember; I was drunk when you met me?" Now he stares off in complete silence. For the first time since the night of my attack, I break down and cry. Out of nowhere, the tears begin to flow uncontrollably and I can't make them stop. Now I'm thinking he must think I'm crazy. He wraps his arms around me and holds me as we both lay there and fall asleep in uttered silence.

"My God, you are so pretty," he tells me. . "I'm going to marry you."

I'm thinking, *pretty? Are you kidding me?* I wore turtlenecks in the summer trying to hide the scars on my neck, and I didn't feel pretty. Bernard and I begin spending more and more time together. I begin to allow him to pay for things, which made him feel like he was my man. Every now and then I would insist and he would let me pay for things. I hadn't notice before but, he was a real gentleman. I began to pay close attention to how he was treating me. He was so patience and caring. I would wake up and find him starring down at me and smiling. Could I really be beautiful to this man? Surely he sees all my scars. *The way he looked at me, begin to bring healing on the inside. He made me feel beautiful! And that's something money can't buy*

At the time, I didn't believe I could fall in love. Bernard says he'd loved me since the first time he saw me. Maybe it's possible, but let me tell you: for me, it wasn't like that. I wasn't interested in Bernard; my mother chose him. You have to remember, I was in a dark place in life at this point. My mother chose him because he would come to the house and visit. He would sit and talk with mom and dad for hours. He would come by and talk with them, even when I wasn't there. He did this for months. I would get tired of his visits and sometimes sneak out the back door when I saw him coming and drive off.

"That's a good boy," my mother said one day. "His mom has raised him well. He's got good manners."

"Well, you date him," I replied. She slapped me so hard!

Bernard's dad was in the navy and was stationed here in Georgia around '83 or '84. His family is originally from Huntsville, Texas. His dad was in the navy and was out to sea most of the time. He lived with his mom, sister, and brother. They were a Navy family and moved around a lot. He tells the story of how he saw me and told his friends that I was going to be his wife. I never knew him before the day at the beach, and after I did, I didn't like him. He wore these huge, military issued, eyeglasses and his mom dressed him funny. He wasn't for me. He was the ugliest guy within a 100 mile radius.

That eventually changed, obviously. Bernard pursued me for a while, although he tells it a little differently. He'd come to the house, and every now and then, when I got bored, I would let him take me out. He was a gentleman. He would buy gas and open doors for me. And we all know it was hard getting a brother to open a door, and you can forget about buying you a little gas. He would do really nice stuff, but I didn't like him, like he liked me. He would always take me out on his paydays and I would let him, knowing I wasn't interested at all. My mom said I was leading him on, and that wasn't right. After a while he got the hint.

He pursued me for a while, but then, he stopped coming. I asked my Mom, "Where'd your boyfriend go?" and she just looked at me like she was going to knock me out. I got in my car—I knew where he lived— I made up my mind that I was going to go find him. I drove by his house three or four times. His mom was outside working in the yard. I knew he was home because his car was parked outside. His mom was outside and that made me a little nervous. She had this little white dog with pink ribbons on its ears and polished toenails. What in the world? What kind of black people put ribbons on their dogs? I should have never stopped but I did. The dog's name was Ashley Nicole McGowan. *That is so crazy*, I thought. *I knew you all were weird, but y'all got a dog with three names?* We had a dog whose name was Cane. No middle name, no last name, just Cane.

Anyway, I passed by his house three or four times. I didn't know how to stop. Finally, I slowed down, and I turned my music down, and I said, "Do you know Bernard?" His mom cussed me out. I'm thinking she didn't even know me, and she just laid into me. I started shaking and pulled over to park. She was telling me he wasn't there, but I knew he was. She was just going off. I was shaking so because of how she was talking to me, and I was just saying, "Yes, ma'am; yes, ma'am." Now I'm wondering what in the world had he told them about me, do she know me, what did I do.

Eventually, she begins to laugh and I feel a little better. You know he lives here, so stop acting crazy, she says. I parked my car, and I went inside. When I get in he is lying on the couch watching TV. I'm just relieved to be out of his mother's sight. When he looks up and sees that it is me he just lights up like a Christmas tree. Never knew I could have that effect on some. I go and sit on the couch next to him.

"Your mom is crazy," I told him.

"Naw," he said, "she's alright."

"No, she's crazy."

"What are you doing here?" he asked.

"Oh, nothing, I just haven't seen you in a while."

"I got the hint that you didn't want to be bothered."

His mother invites me to stay to dinner and I accept. It turned out they weren't too bad. That was the turning point in our relationship. His dad's ship was due to port later in the week and they were all excited. His ship had been out to sea for months and the families of the crew members would get dressed up and make signs for their return. The families would cheer and wave as the ship pulled to shore. They would stand and wait to greet them. It's totally beautiful to see them all hugging and kissing. I listen as his mom plan the dinner menu for his dad's arrival and they super clean the house. The house would be stocked with all his favorite things. It sounded wonderful, as I listen to their excitement.

"You want to come with us?" he asked.

"I don't know y'all like that," I said, but his mom gave me this look. I figured I had better go with them.

"I'd like you to meet my dad"

Looking at his mom, I replied, "Sure, I'd love to come".

We went and stood on Kings Bay, and the ship came in, and that's when things really took off. He would later tell me that his mom and dad both like me. Funny, I didn't get that impression from his mom. I wondered how she treated the people she didn't like, if she was giving me the 'I like you' treatment. After that, I was invited to Christmas dinner and then a family outing in which they took their RV Camper. Bernard bought me a watch that Christmas, and we attend a winter ball. As much as I was enjoying the time with him and his family, I still wasn't hearing any bells. My mom told me that if I didn't like him, I shouldn't take anything from him because that would be leading him on. You know how older women are. I was thinking to myself, there is no way *I'm giving this watch back; mother can say what she wants.*

We kept kicking around for a long while. We head to the mall, and purchase some new clothes. These would be clothes that I like along with some new eyeglasses. What was interesting was that Bernard lived at home with his parents. Most young adults can't wait to get out of their parents' house, or so I thought. He had a job, but he didn't have a girlfriend. Poor guy was taking his paychecks home and leaving them on the dresser in his bedroom. I thought, *this has got to stop right here. Somebody's got to spend his money.* He was so ugly, I guess nobody wanted it.

We started hanging out, and we became more and comfortable with each other. Nobody in my family or any of my friends liked him. Bernard is very outspoken. He's black or white. There are no gray areas with him. It took me a long time to become ok with his personality. As a matter of fact, I learned to appreciate and respect his honesty. I found myself pulling away from anyone who spoke ill of him. We spent a lot of time alone, just the two of us. We formed this intimate covenant thing. The man was good to me and for me and I wasn't about to let nobody mess it up.

I started college in Jacksonville and went to live with my sister Vanessa. Bernard and I would see each other on Wednesday and then again on weekends. We would stay on the phone talking for hours. We would fall asleep talking about nothing. I remember one Saturday, I came over to his house, and his mom had just gotten the telephone bill. It would be cheaper for you to move in than to keep paying these phone bills. She was like him; they would just say whatever ran across their minds. I was always thinking she was going kill me. So I just look over at Bernard.

Bernard called me one night and he seemed really excited to talk to me. He then proceeds to tell me, "I called my dad on the ship. I asked him if you could move in here with me, and he said yes." What in the world? *Ain't anybody going to move in with you?* His mom, who had picked up on the upstairs phone, says, "Monica, you're moving in with us?"

Hold on a minute! This family was happy, while I was thinking "my momma would die" if she heard I moved in with Bernard. She really liked him but, she would never approve of us living together, unmarried. The family began to make room in their home for me, and his mom started buying new things. She wanted me to feel at home, so she brought towels and sheet sets in the colors that I like. She went shopping

MY LIFE, MY FAITH, MY JOURNEY

for the soap of my choice, deodorant, toothpaste and even some of my favorite foods.

I knew I couldn't just move in with my mother less than ten miles away. I began to stay the weekends with them and hope that no one in my family would notice. I am grown! I come and go as I please with no problem. I came every Friday after school and work. I made sure to stay out of sight when I wasn't with family members as to avoid any suspicion. The more I came the more comfortable I got with him. It was like we were married. We open a joint checking account, in which we still have to this day. We begin to combine our money and pay our bills together. We even paid a few bills in the house for his parents. I stop staying in Jacksonville with my sister period. I drove back and forth to Kingsland every day.

I began to get fatigue. School, work and the drive was taking a toll on my body. I would come home and go straight to bed. A coworker suggested I take vitamins and I did for all of a week but, they didn't help me at all. I'm sleeping like a bear every night and I'm not doing any of my homework. I would rush through class assignments while eating lunch and for the most part I was able to maintain passing grades in each class.

We are all sitting around at work waiting for lunch time and I'm yawning, which I began to do a lot of, when a co-worker ask "Monica, when is your baby due".

"What baby" I respond.

She looks at me with more shock on her face than I had on mind, that she had even asked me such a question. "Wait just a minute baby; you mean to tell me, that you don't know you're pregnant?" she questions me.

I forcefully denied any such possibility.

"I tell you what, there's a clinic around the corner, and here's $20.00 for the test. If you are not pregnant, I'm out of $20.00 and I will apologize. But, if I'm right, tell Mr. Bernard I want my money back tomorrow" and hands me the money.

Needless to say, Ms. Judy was right and she got her money back the next day. Having 3 daughters living with her, and all 3 having gone through pregnancies, gave Ms. Judy wisdom beyond my comprehension. Not only was I pregnant, I was 5 months pregnant.

Forget Bernard, my mom is going to just die. Bernard went out and got drunk when I gave him the news, while his mom decides the baby will need things and heads to the local Wal-Mart to shop for her first grandchild; she is overjoyed. She had her own suspicions but, decided not to say anything. Me; well I went upstairs and cried myself to sleep.

I wanted to keep my pregnancy a secret for a little while until I could figure out how to tell my family. Well forget that. This town is too small and people began to talk. My oldest sister, Danette, found out that I wasn't staying with my momma when I came back and forth to Camden and that I wasn't staying with my other sister, Vanessa during the week, like I had preteen to do for months. Danette was coming to kill everything big enough to die at the McGowan's residence. She bang loudly on the door and yelled for me, to open up. Bernard and I open the door and she looks at me. "I'm going to tell Momma you're staying here and you're pregnant!" Thus, Bernard's mom comes to the door and she and my older sister exchange words.

Understand: Bernard's mom and my sister are both the same age. Bernard's family didn't have the Christian values, per se, that we had, so Danette could not understand how a mother could allow her son bring his girlfriend into her home when they weren't married. We all had a few words. I know in my heart that this is not going to be good. Of course, Danette goes to my mom and tells her everything. My mom calls to tell me she is very hurt because she didn't raise me like this. I didn't know what to do or say. I just came to a place where I stopped talking to anyone for a while. I needed to get myself together, so I made plans to find my own place.

Pregnant and confused, I began to look for a place to live. I did things quietly without Bernard knowing. What was our crime? We were both young and in love. Yes, I had fallen in love with him and knew the exact moment when it happened. I was crazy about him and he was crazy in love with me. It didn't happen the way they thought but, it happen and I was happy. He had changed my life. I wasn't depressed any more, I'd completely stop drinking, I was a full-time student and I worked a full-time job. What we shared had cause a complete metamorphosis and no one notice. We were being judged because we were making decisions without the opinions of others.

Chapter 10

Well we found an apartment. Bernard and I moved in together. Shortly after being there and knowing how my family felt about us living together, we talked of marriage. I didn't want to marry because I was pregnant nor did I care about please others. My sisters and brothers had all made mistakes in life and love, so what right did they have to prevent me from the same choices. I knew my family loved me but, I had to make choices for myself even if they did not agree.

Around this time the holidays are approaching, Bernard asked, "Will you marry me?"

"I am not going to marry you," I replied.

But, he remained persistent and asked a couple more times. I finally said yes. My Mom was very pleased. She loved the fact that we were getting married and the baby would have a father. Bernard and I got married December 28, 1989. I was exactly eight months pregnant and had our daughter exactly one month after the wedding. Breon will be twenty-three on January 28 and she continues to change our lives.

Breon was the only child for a while. My children are three years apart. I remember saying to my husband that we needed to have a son, but he didn't want any more kids. Truth be told, we didn't plan for the one we already had. She just kind of caught us off guard. A reality TV show called, *I Didn't Know I Was Pregnant* could have presented me. I was near six months pregnant before I knew she was on the way. We hadn't missed a monthly cycle and except for little weight gain, nothing was out of the ordinary with our first pregnancy. Bernard was adamant about not having any more children so I would have to wait until he could be convinced.

Bernard went out and got drunk when we found out about Breon. He had asked to me to inquire concerning abortions and that he would pay half. His mother was more upset than I was, if you can believe that. She hit the roof! She had become pregnant with him as a teenager and there was no talk of abortion. She hadn't aborted him and just couldn't believe he would even suggest such a thing. He later apologized to me and his family. He just didn't know what he was going to do. He knew his father would expect him to stand up and take responsibility for me and the baby. After all, he was man enough to ask his father if I could move in with him.

Bernard and I get married after moving into our own place. The preacher that I grew up under actually married us. Bishop Dawson comes over and we get married right there in the apartment. I make spaghetti and garlic toast and we drink Kool-Aid. I was nobody's cook back then but, we were married. Bernard and I were both scared. My mother and his mother were both happy.

Being a wife and a new mother brought many changes. I left college because I didn't know how to balance both motherhood and school. All of my dreams were suddenly placed on hold.

When Bernard and I married, we never imagine how our journey through life would test our love. True love will prove itself in the course of life. We would find out according to 1 Corinthians 13: 4-8 that "true love suffereth long, and is kind; love envieth not; love vaunteth not itself, is not puffed up, doth not behave itself unseemly, seeketh not her own, is not easily provoked, thinketh no evil; rejoiceth not in iniquity, but rejoiceth in the truth; beareth all things, believeth all things, hopeth all things, endureth all things, love never faileth.

CHAPTER 11

We had Breon in January. When she was two months old, Bernard's dad convinced him that he needed to join the military so that he could take care of Breon and me. So, he up and joined the military. He comes home and tells me he's joined the military and needs to prepare to leave. He will be leaving for basic training in April. I said, "Well, you go right ahead, because I'm not going anywhere. I didn't tell you to join the army, so you can take your daddy with you." I packed my clothes and headed to my mom's house. My attitude was that he could go ahead without us. I wasn't going with him and I meant it. I've never lived away from my family and wasn't planning to do so any time soon.

"Wait a minute," my mother said. "That's your husband. You have to go where he's going!" I wasn't going and boo-hoo cried about it. My place was with my husband. As his wife, I was to give him every opportunity to take care of his family. After, I finished crying, with no sympathy from my mom, Breon and I headed back home to Bernard.

Bernard joined the army. After basic training, we received orders for Fort Lewis, Washington. We ended up moving to Washington State and leaving Georgia. This is half-way around the world. I'm five days away from home, and in the midst of I-don't-know-where. All I remember is that it rained. No, I mean like every day, it rained. I would call my mom and tell her it was raining. I'd just cry and say, "It's raining," and she would just listen and say, "Oh, Monica."

It got better after we met the couple upstairs, Mary and Pierre. Mary invited me to church, so now I knew someone. She taught me how to catch the bus, no bus in Kingsland, except for the school buses. We only had one vehicle, and Bernard had to use it to go to work. I didn't know the area so I wouldn't know where to go are how to get there anyway. I would sit home all day, with the baby, and wait for him to get off. I felt so all alone. Once I made some friends and started going to church it got better.

I got a job! We were able to purchase a second vehicle shortly afterward and things were looking up. We joined the church were our neighbors were members. I joined the choir and fell in love with first lady, Mary States. She knew I was young, married and far away from home. She invited us over to dinner and immediately became a confidante.

The church taught on prayer and fasting and I was very intrigue. I had wanted a second child but Bernard was not hearing it. I shared this with First Lady States and she gave spiritual insight on how to go about it. She explained that I was to first ask God and whatever He said would be what would happen. My first fast! Three days of water and reading my bible. I prayed and asked God for a son and He said "Yes" by way of a dream. I told First Lady. She said if God said yes, so would Bernard. I patiently wait for the right time to share it with him and of course he has reservations.

"How do you know it will be a boy" he inquires.

"Because I asked God" I replied.

"One more child" he says "and if it's not a boy, then we'll just have two girls".

I immediately agreed. I had complete confidence that I had prayed according to His will and He heard and granted my petition. Evan was born on March 06, 1993.

Two months after Evan was born, Bernard received orders to Korea. The orders were for 1 year, unaccompanied by family. We packed and headed back home to Georgia. Bernard and I had decided that the kids and I would return home to family instead of staying in Washington. Being with family would be better for us while he was absent for a year.

Being apart for a year! How in the world can the military be allowed to do such a thing to married couples? I worried about the separation and prayed within myself. I knew my husband and this was not going to be easy. God can keep you, if you want to be kept.

Chapter 12

We've learned lots of lessons throughout our marriage. The one thing I know is that sometimes it takes someone older, someone with more wisdom, to help you see what you cannot see. There are certain decisions and choices we should make, but because we are not capable of looking in the right direction, the Lord has to use other people, even situations and circumstances, to turn us in the direction we should chose but lack the wisdom to do so. I tell everybody my husband was hand-picked by my mother, but his father also chose me for him. I've heard my father-in-law say he felt I was a young lady with a good head on her shoulders. He saw I had a job, I was in college, and I had my own car, while Bernard saw that I was pretty. I also remember my mother saying, "He's got good values, Monica. His mom raised him well", while I saw that he was willing to buy gas with those un-cashed checks on the dresser.

So, you've got his father choosing me for him, and my mother choosing him for me. Two older people in the picture trying to encourage a relationship between two who would shape the minds of the next generation. I think the wisdom of what they saw—what we couldn't see ourselves—helped a lot. I have a lot of respect for my mother and what she has to say, even in my life now. There are certain situations in which I'll call her and take heed to what she has to say. One thing I know for sure,' the young people have the strength, but the older people have the wisdom, and they know the way. My mother brings a lot of different insight into life circumstances. Especially in marriage and raising children, she's been a tremendous blessing for us. The things I currently struggle with, she's already gone through and freely advises all who have an ear to hear. For every situation, mother takes me to the Word.

CHAPTER 13

One of the things I did with my kids was that, I didn't allow anybody to keep them. My husband and I were watching something on the news about a young man who was molested. His mom would drop him off, with someone who she trusted, and he was being repeatedly molested. Nobody kept my children! I kept my own kids because I didn't trust people. I was from a small town and now living in a big city and things that were happening to children was never heard of. I didn't know enough about people in the city to have anyone caring for my children.

When we were in Washington State, I got a job at the Exchange. The bills were piling up and we needed the second income. I struggled with this for a long time but, decided to give it a try. I guess Breon was about two, we would take her to a lady I had found in our apartment complex, a retired nurse. She was doing home daycare, so I take my baby to her. I will never forget what happen. I turned into her section of the apartments, and my baby would just boo-hoo cry. That disturbed me so, that it was hard to focus on work. I remember sitting in my car, on this one particular day and my cell phone ranged. I picked up the phone and Bernard's mom is on the other end. She could hear Breon crying. I share with her what was happening and how I'm feeling.

"Monica," she said, "she doesn't know how to tell you something's wrong. Crying is the only way a baby can tell us something is wrong. Breon is not a cry baby, she pretty much like everybody."

I put my car in reverse and drove home. I called the Exchange and informed them that I would not be back. I was going to stand on my faith and believe God for provision for my house but, it would not be at the expense of my child.

Later when Bernard returns home, I explain to him what I had done. Let me tell you and believe me when I say 'men and women don't think alike'. All he knew was that we had bills to pay and my income was necessary in order for us to make ends meet.

Breon had cried like that before, but you know, sometimes you think that kids are just being kids. This particular morning, it was like I heard something in her cry that really disturbed me. I didn't have any proof of anything that was being done wrong. The only thing I knew for sure was that my baby was trying to tell me something. After that, nobody ever kept my kids. Nobody! I stayed home with my kids. When my husband and I would go out to celebrate anniversaries and birthdays, they would be right there with us.

CHAPTER 14

My son Evan was a sickly baby. He was born with many medical problems. Bernard had gone to Korea shortly after taking leave and getting us settled in Virginia. We had decided that his mother would be a great help with the children and being near his parents would be best for us. Prior to Bernard's leaving, we didn't know of any of Evans' medical issues. I lived at the military hospital in Portsmouth. Evan cried day and night. I couldn't hold down a job because no one wanted to keep him. My mother-n-law was the only one I was ok with watching him for me. We tried to work alternate shifts so she and I could both have jobs but, that proved to be impossible. Evan was born with hernias, a collapsed lung, and to top it off, he had asthma. We had no idea what was happening and my patience is worn out.

Evan would cry and scream oh, how he would *scream*. I thank God all the time for a praying Mother and a mother-n-law who would bend over backwards for her Grandchildren. One night I became so tired of his screaming, I remember looking down at him and thinking I could just put a pillow over his face. I thought about killing my son because I was exhausted. I was mentally and emotionally exhausted. In the meantime; my husband was in Korea falling in love, which I would find out later.

My in-laws both worked but when they were off, they would take care of him because they knew I was tired. One day while picking Evan up from my in-laws, my father-law asked me to sit down.

"It's not normal for this boy to be crying like this, he says, we've been talking and we want you to take him to a specialist".

"What kind of specialist" I inquired.

"Well, look through the telephone book and lets just start calling and see" he respond.

We began our search and soon found someone we all agreed on. She was from India, and specialized in infants and children health. I call her office and speak directly to her. I tell her about Evan and everything he's been experiencing. She listens carefully to our case then makes an appointment.

Evan and I arrived at her office and I'm handed pages of paperwork to fill out. Evan, of course is crying, and the doctor appears from the back room. She's a beautiful woman with a red dot in the middle of her forehead.

She looks at me and says "Come on back, you can finish that later".

She places Evan on the exam table and removes all of his clothes, pamper included. With her hands, she began to examine him from the soft spot at top of his head down to his big toe. When she gets through with her hand examination I just stand there looking at her, thinking this was weird medicine. Without any blood work, or x-rays, she turns to me and gives her diagnosis.

"I'm going to tell you what's wrong with him, but I don't want you to be afraid," she said, as she looks at me. "Your son has a collapsed lung, and he has a bilateral hernia."

This was just from touching that she knew this, and she began to explain to me her findings.

"There're two small holes here in his groin area. These are fat pockets and that move up and down. They've swollen and can longer move back and forward like there're designed too. That's why he's screaming…he's in pain." She continued. "I'm going to take them out today. I've already notified the hospital; they're preparing the surgery room. They know we're coming."

I'm looking at her, thinking, *huh?*

Within two hours of seeing this specialist, I find myself pacing up and down a waiting room floor, waiting for my son to come out of surgery. I had called my in-laws back at her office and they would attempt to help me reach Bernard over in Korea. The doctor did the bilateral hernia repair herself. After what seems like an eternity, she comes out and informed me that everything went well. Evan was in recovery and I could see him as soon as he was cleaned up and taken to the nursery. A few days later, after all the crying and the swelling went down, we took Evan home, and for the first time, he stopped screaming.

CHAPTER 15

I connected myself to a church in Virginia and they had all called to check on us. My mom had raised us in church, so whenever we would move, I would connect my family to a church. My Pastor during this time was a retired navy chief. Pastor Rucker was his name and somehow he convinced me to join the praise team. The praise team consisted of four people. My pastor said he loved my voice—I guess I was singing louder than I should have been from my seat and he convinced me to come out to rehearsal and give it a try.

The praise team had lost a member and now only three singers, so I joined the praise team. Pastor Rucker wanted me to be a part of it, and he would bring his wife to choir practice just to keep Evan for me during rehearsals. She would take Evan into the youth center and take care of him for me. During church services, he would assign someone to take Evan out because Evan cried all the time. I enjoyed the songs of praise tremendously and would often time drift into a place of peace. I found comfort, peace and strength in praise and worship. There is something about praising the Lord that made me feel better.

As I considered placing the pillow over Evan's small face, the words to a song I loved came to my mind. As I began singing that place of peace overtook me, I fell asleep. The Psalmist declared "I will bless the Lord at all times and His praises shall continually be in my mouth." I was becoming my mother! When times were difficult, she would worship the Lord in songs. Mother had taught me what to do in life, when I was unaware that I was a student in training. I found all that I need and I found it in the Lord.

CHAPTER 16

My daughter's name is Eris Breon McGowan, and my son is Evan Bernard McGowan. Breon' name came from a friend who told me I was pregnant before I knew that I was. Ms. Judy was an older lady that I knew in customer service back in Jacksonville, Florida. Ms. Judy gave Breon a name that had my husband's initials. She called my pregnancy before I knew anything. When I had revealed to Judy and the other co-workers that I was, in fact, pregnant, she started writing names. She came up with the name Eris Breon. I figured I'd give my son the same benefit of having his dad's initials so we named him Evan Bernard.

After Evan's surgery things got much better in order to later get worse. God will never put on us more than we can bear. Bernard and I had been separated for seven months and it took a toll on the both of us. I was falling apart with a sick child while he was falling in love with another woman station with him in Korean. He returned home on 30 days of leave and disappears. At the same time he returned home this other woman did also. His desire is not to be with the family he left behind but to be in the arms of his new love.

His parent and I were all confused and really didn't know what to do after he disappeared. We thought about calling the police. This was not like him to leave and say nothing. We thought he went AWOL because he didn't want to go back and finish the tour in Korea. We all just sit and prayed for a few days, when Bernard decides to return home. He goes to his parents instead of home with me and the children. After confronting his parents, he's made to talk to me.

He arrives at the door with his mom. She announces that she's taking the children with her so we could talk. After they are gone, I'm asked to take a seat on the couch. His face is so serious that it frightens me but, I got to know what's going on with him. I've been anticipating his return. So much to tell him about the children, about me, about everything and he just ups and leave and he takes the car. I need to know what has kept him from me and the children. Lord, please give me the strength to hear and understand. I want to be able to help him in any way possible. I love this man!

"What's going on" I ask.

"I've meet someone else and I'm in love with her" he says while looking downward.

All I see is red! I've been sitting in waiting rooms all across the county with a sick child, trying my best not to lose my mind. I'm sick with worry while he under goes surgery, I can't work a job, and this is the thanks I get from you.

"I've been with her for the last few days, he continues. We meet in Korea and have been together for the last couple months. We came home together and we plan on being together. I told my parents and they told me I had to tell you everything."

The next thing I know, he grabs his face. I slapped him as hard as I could. That would be proven by the pain in my shoulder for the next two to three days.

"You want her then take your black ass to her, she can have you with your dumb ass, and I'm out of here. I can't believe this bullshit."

I stomp my way upstairs, pack bags and head out the door. Bernard just sits on the couch motionless. I speed over to his parents, who know what just happen, walked in without knocking, and retrieved my damn children.

"Do you have any money" his father asked.

In the meantime his mom is bagging up juice, chips, cookies, blankets, everything she could get her hands on to help with the trip. She says absolutely nothing. It appears that she maybe crying.

"Monica, where are you going?"

"Can you wait until morning?"

"Are you going to call your pastor?"

"Don't you want to talk about it?"

Too many damn questions! I got to get the hell out of here.

I don't say a word. I'm numb. I'm speechless. I'm broken.......again.

"We love you, Monica, we love you Breon and Evan" they both say repeatedly as we buckled up and pulled away. I couldn't even return the gestures. I felt nothing.

How can the person that God used to help save you, now turn around and stab you in your heart? There is no pain, like that of a broken heart. A heart that once beat because of love is now dead.

I started toward home. I stopped for gas and to take all the cash from our account. It wasn't much but, I had managed to put aside a few hundred dollars so we could have a good time when he came home. Never thought it would be for this. I didn't want him to have a dime and I really didn't give a damn about him since, he obviously didn't give a damn about me and the children. Let that bitch take care of him. They're in love right? I thought to myself as drove into the darkness of the night. I'm mad as hell and I don't know what I'm going to do nor do I have any idea where I'm going. Anger rest in the bosom of fools. It causes me to make decisions that I otherwise would count up the cost before making.

Not long after stopping for gas, the children fell off to sleep. I can hardly see the road from the crying that has caused my eyes to swell. I'd cried so much that my eyes were all puffy. Neither one of the children understood what was happening and slept peacefully.

I can't go to my mom, she loved Bernard, hell, she handed picked him for me. I can't go to any of my brothers and sisters they didn't like him from the start and would surely want to kill him. As angry as I was, I begin to do what I witness my mother do my entire life. I begin to pray.

"Dear Lord, what am I going to do? These children didn't ask to be born and now they're caught up in our mess. Please Lord, watch over my babies. I'm doing the best that I know. I'm trying to be a good mother. I don't have a book on being a good mother but, I'm trying. I tried to be a good wife. I was faithful to him while he was gone. I went to church like I saw my mother do. I don't smoke or drink. I don't go to the clubs like the other military wives and I don't mess up any of his money. "

"Lord, what did I do wrong?"

"What did I do to deserve this?"

All kind of questions race across my mind, none to which I had an answer. Every emotion took its effect on me as I drove home. I went from anger, to bitterness, from bitterness to resentment and from resentment to the tormenting spirit of rejection.

"Why wasn't I good enough?"

As I drove, I began to sing. "All to Jesus, I surrender; all to him I freely give. I will ever love and trust him, in his presence daily live. I surrender all, I surrender all; all to thee my blessed savior, I surrender all. All to Jesus, I surrender; humbly at his feet I bow. Worldly pleasures, all forsaken; take me Jesus, take my now."

I felt the presence of the Lord as he took his the wheel of my car. I begin to think about all that had taken place and how I had responded. The children were both buckled in and fast asleep. I knew that once morning broke and Breon woke up, she would want to know where her daddy is. We never got to show him the pictures she had made for him. She and granny had made cupcakes and she had made one especially for him. Granny had allowed her to frost and sprinkle one for her daddy and no one was allowed to touch it.

I drove to Jacksonville to my oldest sister, Danette's house. I had called her on the cell, so she was expecting us. I shared with her briefly what had happen and she was highly upset. When I reached the house it was early morning and her husband was up. He hears my car when we pulled up, and lets up the garage. Oh my goodness, I can't believe I made it safely here. All of a sudden, out of nowhere, the tears began to flow. I get out of the car without even turning it off and head to my sisters room. She's still in bed so; I climb in with her weeping like a child. I was wounded and needed a strong shoulder to cry on. Danette is awaken by my tears and immediately respond with hugs and kisses. I try to speak but, I can't. I'm so glad that the Lord speaks tears. He knows what I want to say and can't. The Spirit maketh intercession with groaning's that cannot be uttered. She quiets me until I fall asleep in her arms.

I awake to find myself alone in her bed. She and her husband have fed and bathe the children and are returning from shopping. They are unpacking groceries when I walk to the kitchen. Breon and Evan are both sitting at the table drinking juice and eating.

"Mommy" they both yell out at the same time.

Evan holds out his arm for me to pick him up, while Breon lifts a huge blueberry muffin from her plate for me to see.

"Your in-laws have called twice for you; they are worried about you and the kids; I think you should call them."

"I will…..later, I respond. What time is it?"

With Evan in my arms, I walk over to the guest room. They have unpacked my car and all our things are on the bed and in the closet. I flopped down on the bed and it hits me again; crying uncontrollably.

"I hate him" I said as my sister stands in the doorway.

"Then why are you crying; just take a few days and pull yourself together; you know you're going to have to call momma" she says, all in one breath.

My mother had of way of getting to me like none of her other children. She knew that I would listen because she always advised us with what was written in scriptures. I just didn't want to hear what the bible had to say this time. I wanted to be mad. It was my right and I wanted to indulge. I did manage a call that would be short and to the point. I was leaving my husband because he was seeing another woman and I was not going to be talked out of it. The bible says "to pray for them that despitefully use you" she tells me. I'll talk with you later mother. As if I'm about to pray for that whore.

When I wouldn't take the calls of my in-laws, Bernard began to call. I told my sister to let him talk to the kids but, I really didn't want to talk to him. Breon wanted to go see daddy and granny and begin to ask "when are we going home". She wanted to sleep in her bed, and drive her Barbie car that she had gotten for Christmas. She wanted to know if Pa-Pa had fixed her engine. We would unplug it and tell her the engine was broke when we didn't want to take it outside for her to drive. I assured her that Pa-pa had fixed it and filled it up with gas. I told her the car was parked at the house and Pa-pa made sure no one touched it.

My mother-n-law called on a day when I was home alone. She was excited that I had answered the phone. She wanted to apologize for her sons' behavior and to say how much she missed me and the children. She gave names of people in Virginia that had asked about us and sent greetings. After a while I begin to open up and talk. As a woman, you should never leave your house because of another woman. When you leave, it gives her the opportunity to move right on in, she tells me, and her stuff ain't any better than yours. You need to get back here before you can't come back. My mother-n-law was street wise; she was nothing like my mother. She would tell me things in a way that made as much sense as my mother. She informed me that Bernard was due to leave in a few days. Apparently, he had been lying around doing nothing since the night we left. He had spoken to this other woman a few times on the phone but, she answered one call and cussed her out. They would not be allowed to disrespect her house. She informs me that Bernard had been staying with them because he didn't like being alone at our place. He and his dad had been spending lots of time talking and that he was truly sorry for what he had done.

She was very understanding of how distraught I was and wanted me to know that she and daddy thought I'd been a good wife and mother. They had taken up the idea of going to church on Sundays with me and the children. She didn't want him to leave for Korea without spending time with his kids or them with their dad. She offered to send money for gas or come get them if necessary. She explained that Bernard and I may never get back together but, the both of us would forever be

Breon and Evans' parents. She suggested that we needed to talk to set up financial arrangements for the kids and to properly move from the townhouse we'd be renting.

I make up my mind that I do need to talk to the man and move my things from the townhouse, so I pack our things and head back to Virginia. The kids are excited about seeing their dad and grandparents. We hug and kiss my sister and her husband good-bye. She confesses to me that 'I'm more of a woman than she is, because she would never go back to a cheater.' I guess she's right and that's why she's been married so many times. She could only minister to my pain. She could not comprehend, loving someone after they've hurt you. How often have we hurt the heart of our heavenly Father and he'd forgiven us. I must say, it's far too many times to count.

After promising to call once we arrived, we hit the freeway. Before long, both kids are fast asleep. I turn off the radio and decide to take the drive back to the place I'd called home, in silence. I needed to hear what I was saying to myself inwardly. As I drove down the freeway, I once again begin to sing, I surrender all. I must have hummed for hours, only to be silenced by the waking of children. One woke child would soon wake the other. After stopping for food and gas, we finally arrived home.

To my surprise the house was dark and empty. Someone had parked Breon's car in the middle of the floor and once the lights can on, she ran and jumped in it. I called out and no one was there so I picked up the phone and called my sister to let her know we arrived safely. I went to call my mother-n-law but, paused because I didn't know if Bernard was with her, and I didn't want him to know we were back. So, I walk back out to the car to make the call from the cell and he answers the phone. I'm totally silent. I hadn't heard this voice in a while.

"Monica is this you" he says.

"Where's your Mom", I asked.

"You made it home?" he asked.

"Where's your Mom", I repeat.

"Oh, you don't want to talk to me?" he asked

"Is she there or not; I quipped, can you please put her on the phone?"

"I want to talk to you. Please, can you give me one minute; I need to talk to you"

"I don't want to talk to you" I nastily replied.

"Well you don't have to talk. Can you please, just listen then? I'm sorry for my actions. I'm sorry I hurt you and my family. I talked with my dad and he and my mom are very disappointed with me. I've been doing a lot of soul searching and I asked the Lord to please forgive me. I told my dad what I had done and he suggested that I ask you to forgive me too. I messed up! I know I hurt you but, I love you and if you just give me another chance Monica, I won't hurt you again."

"Just tell your mom to call me" I say softly and hang up the phone.

As I walk back toward the house, I can hear the phone ringing from inside. I wipe my tears and speed up to answer it before whoever's calling hangs up. "Hello, hello" I yell but, no one responds. I sit down on the couch and look around at all the furniture that needs to be moved. The kids have pulled out their toys and are playing with them when I pick up the remote and click the television to on. I start flipping from one channel to the next when Barney appears and I know that's it because Breon holler's out "Barney." I sit the remote back down on the table. As I focus across the room, I notice a dozen red roses on the dining room table. I walk over to the table and there's a card with a ribbon on the table. I pick it up and open it. Inside is a hand written note from Bernard. As, I read it, I begin to weep and take a seat in one of the chairs.

The kids are watching TV and playing with their toys, while I'm sitting at the table crying quietly, when I hear keys in the door. The door hadn't even been open but, Breon jumps up and yells "Daddy, my daddy" and heads towards the door with Evan in tow. Sure enough it's him! Bernard opens the door and lifts her in the air. He pushes the door close with his leg and lifts Evan in his other arm. Evan is much younger and really don't know who Bernard is, he just does what he see his big sister doing. Evan was three months when he left and he's been gone for seven months. I kept his picture on tables to help them remember him but, Evan was too young. I stand to my feet, as I turn my back to him and walk over to the couch.

Breon is the spitting image of my Bernard's mother. If you saw the three of us together, you would swear my mother-n-law was her mother and I was a relative. She is the first grand in my husband's family. Once we knew that I was having a girl, they brought diamond earrings. My father-n-law was told it was a girl while out to sea. On one of the stops the ship made, he went abroad and brought diamonds for her. When the ship pulled in, we all go out to meet the sailors and my father-n-law hand me a little white box with diamonds. It's his first time seeing his granddaughter and he hugs and kisses her all the way home. I look at the ring on my hand, then back at the earrings. All I have is a facsimile of a diamond, and this child gets a karat for each ear?

Bernard's mom treated Breon like she was her own. As a matter of fact, my oldest sister, thought it necessary to stop by and tell her that Breon was not her baby; she was my baby. Breon spent more time with her grandmother than she did with me because my mother-in-law said I didn't know what I was doing, which was true. I didn't; I had never had a baby before. We never worried when we were out; we knew she was safe and being spoiled. It wasn't until after Bernard joined the service, that we were able to really practice parenting. By that time she had set a standard on how she wanted her granddaughter to be cared for.

Evan is the spitting image of me and my father. He has since grown to look more like his father than anyone ever would have expected. By the age of fourteen, there were signs of a full beard. We lived in Washington State when Evan was born. Once we came back to the East coast, my mother-n-law ruined him too. They were and still are a true blessing to the all their grandchildren. They could afford to buy things for them that Bernard and I was in no position to purchase. They always had the best of everything.

As I watched sat on the couch watching Bernard and the kids playing, all kinds of thoughts ran through my mind. I never thought I would have to raise them without him. I never would have asked God for a son if I knew I'd be one day considering divorce. Evan was just 1 year old and Breon was just four when Bernard came to visit from Korea. We both interact with the children but say nothing to each. The doorbell sounds and Granny appears from the shadow. She had been given a key to assist with the children used it often. "It's my Granny" Breon yells. And the celebration starts over again. You would have thought we've been gone for years instead of the few weeks we spent in Florida.

Bernard asked if we could go to dinner. We need time to talk and make arrangements for what was next. I agreed and we did. The evening went smoothly but, I was not about to make it easy for him at all. We both get to-go trays as neither one of us have much of an appetite. The car ride home is painfully silent. All I could think about was what she looked like, did she know he was married, was she with him when we had talked on the phone, did she know about the children? Can I even ask these types of questions and get an answer from him? He'd probably just lie and I won't add hurt to injury. Once we returned home, he pulls me to his lap and picks up the phone. I pull away but, he forces me to sit and insist he must do this. He dials as I'm forced to listen.

"Hello Sherri, he says. I'm here with my wife. I needed to call and tell you that I can't see you or talk to you again. I love my wife and children and I always will. I'm sorry if I hurt you but, we walked into this with our eyes wide-open. You knew I was married to Monica and we had two children when we meet. I didn't hide anything from you. I was over there lonely and missing my family and you made yourself available. My wife is here because I wanted her to witness me burning this bridge. If my wife decides to stay with me or not, you and I still will never be together. I've hurt too many people that I love and love me and will spend the rest of my life, if necessary, trying to help with the healing. Please say whatever you have to say now because this will be the last time we have any contact. No, this isn't love; he says in response to her, this is lust, not love. I'm in love with my wife. I'm praying God will heal us and restore our marriage. I hope you have a good life" he says then hangs up.

Wow! I could see how hard this was for him but, it was something he felt in his heart that he had to do. For real healing to take place, he had to close every door. Forgiveness is not easy but, with God all things are possible. I hear and see all that he is doing but, it's just not enough. I fall into deep depression. Bernard tries to get an extension of his leaves but, to no avail. He misses his return flight and we find ourselves in another mess. He is now considered AWOL and has to pay for his returned flight back to Korea. His dad is still disappointed with him and refuses to loan him the money. When his dad refuses to help, I realize just how upset he is with Bernard. They were really disappointed with him and refused to help even knowing he could go to jail. I'm hurt but, I know he needs to return to work to take care of his family. I call my big sis, Danette, and she purchases a ticket for him to return. Danette loved me more than she hated the man that I was married too. Bernard goes back to complete his tour of Korea and returns with orders for Fort Meade, Maryland. And once again, we have to move.

We arrive to Fort Meade and within a week of living in the base hotel, is granted government housing. We settle into our home on Baker Street and I enroll Breon in school. I've made a personal decision to work so

I would never have to completely depend on no one but, the Lord. I'm relentless as I begin looking for a job. I begin working at the exchange within a few months of being in Maryland. My supervisor is very active in her church and invites me and my family to come for a visit. She has a beautiful spirit and she and I connect immediately. We visit and I instantly fall in love with her Pastor. Pastor Jackie is a powerful, petite, older white woman but, she's anointed to teach the word with power and clarity. The church has such a Spirit of Excellence that I know I want to join after only a few visits. I ask my husband for permission to join and he says "yes." I make the necessary plans to join during the very next service. I volunteer to help with children ministry and books/tapes store. Bernard came on special occasions like Christmas and Mother's Day. If any sport game was on TV, he was on the couch watching it.

I begin going to marriage counseling. Bernard declared he didn't need it and I didn't feel it was my place to insist. I lived on this emotional roller coaster and went to get help for Monica. Some days I was up, some days I was down. The trust was broken in my marriage and I didn't know how to deal with it. I loved him but the process of forgiveness would take time. I couldn't talk about my feelings without him blowing up. If you forgive someone, then you shouldn't bring it up. He was right! But, my soul was wounded and the bleeding didn't stop. How dare you cut me then refuse to let me bled. At night he would make love to me then fall off to sleep while, I lay weeping silently. I function robotically and no one knew but me and the Lord. Where do you go when your soul is wounded?

Shortly after learning of the affair, I left. A few days after I returned from my sister's, he had to head back to Korea. We really didn't have time to mend the brokenness that had taken place. He was in one place and I was in another and let me tell you from experience, 'you can't heal if you're apart'. Coming to Maryland would be the first time we'd lived together in over a year. I wasn't good at expressing myself and my husband was worst. Silence often took over when we were alone.

So much to say but, not knowing how became obvious to me. So once again, I took to writing. It was therapeutic with side effects, or so I thought.

I poured myself into church, work and the kids. I cooked, clean and did everything expected of me by my husband but, inside I was dying. I stop drinking but, would still buy alcohol for him when I shopped. I stop going out to clubs and withdrew myself from couples events that we usually took part in. Church had become my past time outside of work and the kids and Bernard seemed to not care at all. We were given his and hers KJV bibles for Christmas by his parents and I begin reading every day. I had a bible but, these were much nicer. I read in order to deal with the fact that he was still going out and he was still drinking. It's amazing how life goes around; he once hated it when I would drink and now I find myself hating him for doing it.

I spent many nights unable to sleep when he would go out. I would lay awake upstairs in bedroom with the kids fast asleep and wait for the lights from his car to flash across the bedroom walls. Once home, I would pretend to be sleep as he crawled into bed next to me. I could smell the smoke from the club on his clothes and the alcohol on his breath. As messed up as I was, I would always pray and ask the Lord to cover him. I didn't want anything bad to happen to my children's daddy. Depending on how much he drank while out, he would either fall asleep or he would be all hands.

I read the entire bible within six months. On this particular night, Bernard comes home after being out and he reeks of alcohol. He climbs into bed and he's all hands this night. I had been in revival all week and prepared my heart for a miracle. Each night I sowed a specific amount and wrote on my offering envelope. This was something I'd never done nor seen done. I begin to put a demand of the Word of God and would fine out this night that 'His word will not return void.' Bernard falls asleep as I lay weeping softly on my pillow, when all of a sudden the supernatural presence of God fills my bedroom. I'm lifted from my bed and bent over in the fetal position. I never see a face but, His presence was simply awesome. All I could do was worship, like I had never worshipped before. The peace of God that surpasses all understanding invaded my entire being. My intellect struggled with my spirit but, my flesh had to surrender to. It was powerless against the Holy presence. I was having an out-of-body experience. I knew I was naked, I knew that I was on the floor, I knew I was upstairs in my bedroom and I also knew that I was in the presence of something phenomenal.

Once I perceived the peace of His presence; I completely gave in. All I could do and wanted to do was worship. To fully comprehend, that I had granted access to His presence was mind-boggling. This supernatural presence brought total completeness. I felt whole and needed absolutely nothing. Oh how I longed to stay and never leave this place. The sound of water flowing became vocal.

A voice as majestic as the quiet river streams spoke "Tell them; tell them about my peace" He says.

"Tell who" I humbly replied.

"Every one that you meet, tell them about this peace. My peace have I given unto you. Walk in the authority that's given you by My Spirit. Take authority over every evil force that come against your life. I've endowed you with power and confidence; speak my word and watch it preform when you speak it in faith. The same way you did on that cold night in Carolina."

I open my eyes and take a slow glance around the room. I look over at Bernard but, he's sound asleep. I can't believe he did hear that. I slowly pull myself up from the floor. I try to make sense of what just happen as I simultaneously confirm within myself that I'm been restored. I feel alive. I feel powerful. I feel bold. I feel new. As I stand to my feet, I find myself walking over to the closet. I wrap my arms around the clothes that are hanging and boldly declare "You will never go into another club." I fall to my knees, with my arms stretch as wide as possible, touching every shoe in arms reach and again with the same boldness repeat "You will never go into another club" I walk from my bedroom to my daughters' room, then to Evans' room, then downstairs; decreeing and declaring "No weapon formed against me shall prosperous; my marriage is blessed, my children are blessed; the Lord is my shepherd." I walked each hallway, demanding "every unclean spirit, demonic force out. I command you to flee in the name of Jesus. I plead the blood of Jesus."

The next morning, I wake refreshed and on the couch. I prayed myself to sleep. Everything went on as normal. I had changed and I knew it. What I didn't know was the changed that had taken place in me, would cause change around me. I had peace and it had nothing to do with the Holidays. Christmas was coming, the snow was falling and I was no longer bond with depression.

We finished early with the Christmas shopping and all the gifts were wrapped and under the tree. I worked the early shift on Christmas Eve. I would afterward head home to start cooking Christmas dinner for my family. The exchange had been extremely busy all week but, today was the busiest. I clock out, wish my co-workers a Merry Christmas and head home to my family.

I arrived home to find Bernard watching a football game with a friend he'd invited over. Breon has a cold so she's lying on the couch half asleep, while Evan plays with toys that are scattered around the room. I hurry upstairs to change into my sweats and back down to start dinner. I offer my husband and his guest drinks as I inquire of the children's eating habits. I take Breon's' temperature then give her a little more Tylenol and a cup of juice.

I move to the kitchen to start the cooking. I reach into the refrigerator and grab the carrots. As I close the door, I take heed to my work schedule that hangs by a magnet on the door. I run for the phone and call back to the store. I ask for my supervisor. Upon hearing her voice I inform her that I had accidently clocked out an hour earlier than I should of and sincerely apologized. I then offered to return if she wanted me too.

"Baby your home now; don't worry about coming back for one hour; go ahead and enjoy your family; and Merry Christmas." She says and then hangs up.

I returned to my kitchen, grabbed a carrot and starting shredding it for my carrot cake. I'm standing there shredding and humming when I hear Bernard scream my name from the front room.

Evan stops playing; lays on top of his sister and stop breathing.

"Daddy, something is wrong with Evan" Breon tells her dad.

Bernard goes over and picks him up. Evan is limp. He's not moving, he's not talking, he is not responding at all. Bernard begins to shake him and he still doesn't respond. Now he's screaming my name, "Monica".

I can tell by Bernard's voice that it's urgent. I drop the carrot and hurry out to Living room. When I enter the room, Bernard is holding and shaking Evan. I move over with my arms extended and he gives him to me. His eyes and ears have darkened. I can tell from the darkness of his complexion that he's not getting in oxygen.

"Jesus, Jesus, Jesus" I cried out.

"Call 911, I scream to my husband and his friend. I'm immediately aware of the seriousness of this matter, as well as my helplessness. I remember my mother; calling on the name of Jesus. There are no other options!

"Lord, I don't know what to do; help me, show me what to do, please Lord" I pleaded.

I sat on the floor, tilt back his head and scooped his mouth. I had to make sure he didn't swallow something. "Nothing is in his throat, I respond." It's no longer me but, the Holy Spirit, which had taken over. I begin to administer CPR without ever having taken a class. I breathed 3 short breaths into his mouth then, I carefully thrust his small chest three times. I repeated the process as I watch two grown men unable to dial 911.

"Give me the phone" I yelled.

"This is 911" a male voice says

"My baby isn't breathing; please help me; I begged, just tell me what to do."

"Madam, help is on the way; you're at 5013A Baker Street right?" he asked

"Yes, please send some help, tell me what to do, he's not breathing" I pleaded.

"What's the baby doing, what happen?"

"He's not breathing; he was ok one minute and then just stops breathing"

"Look at his stomach; is it going up and down?

"No he's not breathing, tell me what to do"

"Look in the back of his mouth, is anything there"

"No, I've already done that. I'm giving him breaths and chest compressions. Is anyone coming?" I screamed.

"Ugh" Evan begins to gag and cough.

"He's throwing up" I yell into the phone.

"That's a good thing the operator says; they're turning onto Baker Street now; tell me when you see them"

"Please hurry; I don't want my baby to die; I see them" I cry out as I move towards the front door with Evan in my arms.

The passenger door swing open and a male paramedic run over to me and take him from my arms.

"He was fine one minute and all of a sudden, he stopped breathing" I explained.

"Madam, please move back, and let us take over" He insist.

Evan is carried into the ambulance. I notice my slippers are wet from being outside in the snow, when I hurried upstairs to change them and grab my coat. I rush back downstairs and wait for the doors of the ambulance to open. Once open, they asked if we were going to ride with them or drive our personal car. I jumped immediately onto the ambulance with my baby while instructing Bernard to call our sitter for Breon and meet us at the hospital.

Well the sitter wasn't home, so Bernard brings Breon with him to the hospital. It seems like we were there for hours before the doctors finally came out to talk with us. Evan apparently had a fibroid seizure. The seizures are brought on by a high fever. And these fevers show up out of nowhere. The child is ok and then he's not.

Shortly after this traumatic event, I decide to leave my job. I wasn't about to trust anyone, including my husband with the life of my son. This episode with Evan caused me to look at every aspect of my life. I told inventory of where I was and where I had come from. I stood and for the first time, remembered the days of old.

I began to read the Word and apply it to my life like never before. I began to confess the Word in my house, over my marriage and over my life. I picked up the phone one Friday evening. I wanted my mother to know that I was saved and that my life was in God's hands. Whatever He wanted for me; I wanted for myself.

I became faithful to my husband and to my children like never before. I made then priority in my life. I chose to read my bible rather than watch TV and made going to church mandatory for me and the children. I became so consumed with the Word that I begin to prophesy to my husband what I felt was next for my life.

"We are going back home to Georgia, and I'm going to start a ministry. We are going to build a house from the ground up. This house will have white cabinets with gold handles and green carpet. I will stand before rooms filled with people and they will listen to what I have to say concerning the things of God."

Any time I talked like this, my husband would get silent, and just listen.

"God is going to open a door for you to take us home. When we get there, He will have people in place to help us with the house. This will be a faith walk, so if you don't believe it, then don't say anything.

Breon was a very good kid and was very smart. While up North in Maryland, she attended Odenton Christian School. She was a blessed child because my husband's parents had the means to give her many things that she probably wouldn't have gotten if it was just us.

Late 1996, the kids and I returned home to Georgia. Bernard had received orders for Jacksonville and we were headed home. He would stay behind a few weeks to pack up our things and wrap up all our lose ends. He even attended church without me and the kids.

I was so excited to be home. My children knew nothing of living in Georgia and I wanted them to experience life in the country. After settling into an apartment, I begin going to church with my mom. She was delighted to have us home and back at church, as well as my childhood church family.

I enrolled Breon in the public school system. Because of her scores we were advised to attend a school outside of our district. This meant that I would have to drive her to and from school. Shortly after being in school, she tells me that she is being teased by the other kids. The kids picked on her because she talked proper. I told her they were all jealous because they weren't able to pronounce properly. I was teased when we got to Washington because I talked country. She lightens up when I shared my story and decided her mommy was right. When they teased her she would ask them to say the three little words I gave to her; street, straight and strong. No more problems with that, needless to say.

Once Bernard arrives and settles in, we decide to place Breon back in Christian school. There is only one in the area, so we enroll her. We settle into our new home and Bernard starts working in Jacksonville. He soon locates a church in which we both are comfortable. This brings a sense of wholeness to our lives.

We would stay in Georgia for two years before getting orders to move. We have settled on a church that we both loved and agreed on. Our pastor is female and she pours herself into both my husband and me. We were both ordained into the gospel ministry in 1997 and from this season, our spiritual lives would be birth out. Pastor Ethel would speak things in my ears that I now walk in and posse.

We begin to live between Kingsland and Savannah, Georgia. We both hated leaving our church home and searched for alternative to avoid the move. Nothing happen, so we had no choice but, to move to Savannah. Once in Savannah, we begin to have church service in our home. We were faithful to the order of service we had implemented and esteemed it a vital part of our lives.

While living in Savannah, the 911 attacks took place. My husband received orders and had to spend several months overseas. We decided that the best thing for me and the kids was to return home and we did. Upon returning home, I continued the home church services. I would visit a local church twice each month but, for the most part, I keep on doing what was in my heart. After a few months of being home, I began to invite friends and family over for bible study. The attendance grew and I knew that I would soon need a place big enough to accommodate all who wanted to attend.

As I took inventory of all that was happening in my life, I begin to question God as to His purpose and plan. I was lead to an empty building in the downtown area of the city. I explain to the owner that I had no money and really no members. He gave me the building and explained that the first two months were free but, that he expected payment afterward. I agreed and things began to fall in place.

"Lord what would you have me say to your people?" I asked, prayerfully.

All I know is what I had experience in my own life. I would soon find out, that that's all I need to know. My testimony of how the power of God had rescued me would prove itself to be infallible.

I sat and remember the awesomeness of His power in my own life. How as a child, my mother had taken me to the house of God when I was ill and the Elders had anointed me with oil and prayed over me. How I was robbed, kidnapped, raped, stabbed repeatedly and left for dead, how God had sent me home early from work in order to assist Him in saving Evan's life. When I look back over my life, I realize that He had been there all the time. He never left me nor forsake me. When I wasn't thinking about Him, I was on His mind.

CHAPTER 17

The most surprising thing to me about raising my own children is that they're very expensive. You really do have to give up your life so that they can have a life. When I met my husband, I was college student. After we got pregnant, I discontinued college, but I made sure that my husband got a degree. Because of the G.I. Bill, he was in a position to further his education and I was in a position to help him. I gladly tell everyone that his name maybe on it but, it belongs to the both of us. Bernard and I were able to achieve an associate's degree and then a bachelor's degree. We then decide we're too close to stop now and continue to study. He received his MBA, of which we are both extremely proud. He was able to take online courses, and because he worked 12 hours days, I was task with ensuring the work was timely. We did really well. I would prepare assignments but, he had to present them to the class, therefore he had to study also.

As for me, I had to put my dreams of college on hold for a while. I wanted my children to have the best life that we could possibly give them. Being a parent, you do give up a lot so that your children can compete in an ever changing society. I don't think anybody will ever fully understand until they become a parent themselves. You're always ensuring your children have everything they need, even if you have to do without. One Scripture clarifies this for me. "His thoughts are not our thoughts; His ways are not our ways." I think in the long run, when we look at it, we don't lose anything by having children. Blessed is the man whose quiver is filled with children, for they are our inheritance. I believe the Lord orders our steps through life. We have to give up our plan and except his plan for our lives.

I am the pastor and founder of Eagles Wings Ministries. I have been pastoring for twelve years. I never saw this coming. If someone would have asked me 15 years ago, what I thought I would be doing at this stage, it would NOT be pastoring. I worked for Coach Leather Company; I fell in love with their products. I worked in Human Resources at the distribution center in Jacksonville, Florida. My vision was to make it to the corporate level and become 'Miss Coach.' I still love their products to this day. Every purse that I have now is Coach and I continue to remain faithful to the product. I saw myself moving up the corporate ladder and being a national representative. With this vision I would also be able to sustain my home and my husband could leave the military. I could take care of us while he found a job that didn't demand we keep relocating every 3 years but, it didn't happen that way. One day while working at Coach, I'm in the records room on my knees separating files when I heard a voice, clear as a bell, say to me, *Quit*. I remember thinking, *okay, devil, I rebuke you*. You don't just walk away from a job like this.

I had developed a lifestyle of prayer and fasting. A few days each week, I'd turn my plate down and fast. I knew that prayer work and prayer and fasting together work even better. Why wait for problems to arise in order to fast? I need strengthening before the problem ever manifest. In a season of fasting, I'm at home praying when I heard, "Pastor." Be careful what you ask the Lord for because He will answer. I wanted to advance at Coach and begin to pray 'Lord let your will be done in my life.' I thought, *okay, no*, and I kept on living like I didn't hear "Pastor." I am a witness that He will bring us into alignment with His predestine will for our lives. He allows His permissive will, but, then there's His perfect will. We are permitted to do what we want for a season. The divine will of God will shift everything in the atmosphere in order to move us where we should be instead of where we want to be. When it really comes down to the truth of life you've got to do what you were created to do. As Believers, we must know that our human will is powerless to the sovereign will of God.

I tell my husband, "I think the Lord is calling me to pastor." It sounded crazy coming out of my mouth, and I knew it had to sound crazy going into his ear, because this was something we had NEVER discussed. We often talked about my being corporate at Coach and him making officer in the military. We had discussed tithing and being active in church but, not on this level. I share what I had heard with him, and he doesn't respond at all. He just looks at me! Please understand, at this point in our lives, we are doing better than most. I was making as much money as he was and with bonuses. He didn't say anything for a long time, and I refuse to nag him because this was not my idea. To be at the mercy of people is not desirable and the weight of responsibility is enormous. I also understood God to be a God of order. If this was really His will, He would do a work inside my husband. He would cause my husband to come into agreement with His word spoken over my life. I will not live in a divided home. Division leads to frustration and home needs to be a place of peace. Home is where you can find peace from the chaos of the world. I told my husband what I heard and he neither agreed nor did he disagree. He remained silent and that too was ok with me. Months passed and neither of us brought up the subject.

Little did I know; the Lord was quietly working. We never see Him working but, He is constantly performing His word over our lives. In the middle of the night, my husband wakes me. My first thought is he's sick and may need to go to the emergency room. He shakes me and I sat up in the bed. He is holding his head and looking down, when he softly begins to speak.

"Monica," he says sitting on the side of the bed. "If we're going to do this, I don't want to hear you complain. You're going to live off my salary."

"What are you talking about?" I said, and rubbed my eyes.

"If you're going into ministry; we are going to live off what I make, and you are not going to complain."

"Okay" I whisper.

To be entirely honest, this was the last thing I wanted hear him say. I could not do ministry without my husband permission. He now takes away the only excuse I have for not being obedient. With Bernard in agreement, I'm forced to take a long hard look at this thing. Did we fully understand the cost of our yes? No, we had no idea but would soon find out. This move would not only damage our income but, our credit scores as well. Why does God chose messed up people? He must have someone more qualified than me. I've been kidnapped, robbed, raped, stabbed, and cheated on. Lord, why would you send me to your people? He would later respond "because I can trust you with them. I broke you in order to use you. I allowed these things so you would have evidence when I placed you on the stand in the courtroom of life. In every situation, you've turned to me."

CHAPTER 18

I began the ministry in our home. I informed my daughter that she was my missionary and my usher. Evan was my deacon and our treasurer. The kids were excited to be a part of ministry with grown up positions. Honestly we were all clueless as to what we had embarked upon. We began to sing and to worship right in our home. Evan would take a bowl from the kitchen and lift the offering. I made sure everyone had an offering before services would start. As time progress, my husband was inclined to register with the IRS and establish a bank account for deposits. As much as I hate to admit it; what we had started in our home, would prove to be something much greater than we could have imagine.

When we would go out on the town, we often ran into people who we knew and who knew us. Some inquired about our church affiliation and would drop in on our services. I insist they remain faithful to their own church. As we began to share what we were doing, our attendance begins to increase. There were no rules to participate in any of our services. The people were allowed to come as you are. We didn't care about race, religion, addictions, sicknesses, education or anything that would discriminate. We just wanted people to know that salvation is for everyone.

One Sunday, after Bernard had gone back to Iraq; I'm lying in bed. I have this strong sense of urgency to go search for a possible location for the ministry. I get up and ride through town just looking at vacant buildings. On one hand it makes sense but, then on the other hand it doesn't. I really don't have members. We had never offered the right hand of fellowship to anyone for membership. This is something that would need my immediate attention. I keep driving and looking but nothing grabs my attention. On one particular drive, I get a strong urge to pull over. I park and just look around. *What do you see?* Over to my left, I see a brick building with four empty units. The building is old but, it was made of bricks. My dad thought bricks were much better than wood when it came to buildings. I recall being a child and walking to this location. Our local drugstore and grocery store once occupied theses spaces. My mother would buy our groceries from here. Back then she would sign for them and dad would pay once he came home from the road. I sat wondering who owned them now. My mother would know, so I head towards her house.

"Mother, do you know who owns those old brick buildings downtown?" I asked.

She began to tell me who once own them, and the year they passed away. With the last names she recalls, I grab the phonebook. I make two calls before I find the right person. He invites me over to his office.

I walk in and decide to stand instead of taking the seat that is offered. "Mr. Bobbie," I told him, "I need your buildings. I'm getting ready to start a ministry, but I have no members and no money."

"Well, you're going to have to give me something, gal." He sat back in his chair, and he looked at me. Silence dominated the air and I felt as if I couldn't breathe. I wish I have sat down! "I'll tell you what I'm going to do." He says as he reaches for the phone on his desk.

He picked up the phone and called Bobbie Jr., who turns out to be an attorney. As I sit and put things together, I realize that his son and I went to school together. He played football with Bernard during high school.

"He tells Bobbie Jr. to write up a lease contract." I would stop by later in the week and sign the lease agreement. I paid nothing for the first few months. The funds that we did have would be used for paint, chairs, curtains and flower arrangements.

Our lease agreement was written and signed in 2002. Within a few months we were able to pay rent. We have not missed a payment nor have we been late in almost twelve years. We start and continue to walk by faith every day. It's been a blessing as well as a challenge. We started with one unit. As the ministry grew we had to take another. A few years later our membership continued to increase. We began talks of purchasing the property. This would be the greatest step of faith that I'd ever considered outside of my home. Ministry matured from my den and a kitchen bowl, to something I'm so proud of. It's such a beautiful place. We recognize the hand of God as His glory radiates our place of worship. Except the Lord build a house, they that labor; labor in vain.

CHAPTER 19

Along the pathway of faith, of course, I had doubts, and I had fear. I had no money. I recall my home being without electricity on two occasions. I remember going to my sister's house to take a bath because my water had been turned off. There were times when we took from our house to ensure the ministry ran properly. When I didn't pay my mortgage or light bill, it was because I had to make sure that the church was taken care of. We had to walk through seasons of lack and remain content while doing so. Lack became our ground of proving. I clearly recall not having cable, Internet, or cell phones. We had to make a lot of sacrifices for the Kingdom.

I remember pulling up near a gas station with my gas light on, and my son, who didn't know any better, said, "Mommy, the gas light is on. We need to get some gas."

I remember thinking, *okay, but I don't have any money.*

Evan said, "Write a check!"

"It doesn't always work like that," I said. "You have to have money in the bank to write a check."

I walked into the store and purchased two loaves of breads. The corner store had the best bread prices and I always had just enough to make the purchase.

We struggled! My husband and I firmly believed we were doing what God had called us to do, and remained diligent and faithful. I even managed; somehow, to not complain. I cried myself to sleep many nights. I had experience the power of God working in the lives of so many, when He seemed to have forgot us. What in the world had I gotten my family into, I often wondered. McDonald's would have hamburgers and cheeseburgers for forty-nine cents on Wednesdays; we couldn't afford 49 cents. The kids would say, "Mom, can we go get some hamburgers?" and I would think to myself, *we don't even have the forty-nine cents for a hamburger.* I would make spaghetti for dinner without ground beef.

We went through a lot, but we kept the faith, and in return, God has blessed us.

My children learned to embrace the vision, and now have tremendous respect for the dedication we exemplified. Before we moved out in ministry and did anything, Bernard and I had a meeting. We didn't just meet with our kids, but also with my mom and my brothers and my sisters. We began to share with them what we believed God had called me to do. I wanted them to know, just in case somebody in our small knit community was to ask questions. I Informed Breon and Evan how hard it would be at first but, God was going to bless us if we stay faithful. Breon was ten, and Evan was seven when we moved the ministry from home to the front street. I told them that it was going to be real hard, but I assured them that it's not going to be hard forever. I ask that they would bear with us while we do walk in obedience to what God called us to do.

They had to give up cable, as well as going out to dinner and seeing movies. They had become accustomed to going to the movie theater on Friday nights. Every Friday, we would go to dinner and see a movie, or we would go to dinner and bowling. Unless something major was happening, we would always go out on the weekend. My husband and I both worked and together our income allowed us privileges that we would have to give up. We'd go to Kmart and Wal-Mart and shop for no reason. At Blockbuster we would buy more movies than we rented. We went through a season where the movies that we had purchased, would be watched over and over again. This we did for nearly two years.

The thing that really helped the kids during this season was my husband and I was content. We seem excited as we watch movies with them. We learned that our attitudes played a major role in how our kids behaved during these difficult times. If you don't complain about the things in which you have no control over, then you prevent not having things to control you. You having a good attitude concerning difficult seasons, will always have a positive effect on those in your house. I had come to a place of contentment. Even though there were days I wanted to complain, like when we didn't even have basic stuff like soap. Some days we used laundry powder to wash dishes and take a bath. When the kids wanted to do things with their classmates and they could not because we didn't have the five dollars needed to participate. I felt bad as a Mom. I did not like not being able to give to them. Then again, how can I? We were living pay day to pay day. I found myself waiting on my husband's pay days, to purchase basic necessities.

CHAPTER 20

There have been so many times when I've wanted to give up. That happens even now! Even now, there are seasons that I must walk through and I want to give up, because it's a hard place to be in. The problems change but, there are still mountains that I have to climb. My children are young adults now and both college students. I'm not just dealing with the issues in my house, but I'm going to the house of God and dealing with the issues of other people. The office of a Pastor, calls for a very special person. This person must be willing to lay aside their life and be available to those who may be in need. Within myself, I know that I am nothing but, with God working through me, I become a representative of Heaven. What seems minors to one person, may be major to another. As a pastor, you serve as a Word-based counselor, or an advisor. Pastors have to wear many hats to in order to assist those they've been sent to minister too. *Many people will listen and take your advice simply because you're a Pastor. What a delicate and sensitive place to stand. Knowing that the words you speak carry great weight is a responsibility within itself.*

You must always be open and understanding to the situations of others. The main goal is to convinced folks to trust in the Lord. Your assignment is to turn their heads in a different direction to see things a little differently than they often time appears. Things are not as bad as we've convinced ourselves they are. As a pastor, I deal with a lot of personal matters that I've had to go through myself. I stand as a witness that God will take care of His own. During the storms of life is where He proves Himself. The storms come to show us who He really is and what He can do if we only have faith and believe. *As a Pastor, many believers are under the false impression that I don't have problems. I'm somehow exempt from all the cares of life. I need people everywhere to know that "Life is happening to all of us", no one is exempted.*

Every now and then, I find myself questioning the work I'm doing; is it worth it? Am I making a difference? Is anyone getting it? Eventually somebody will show up and informed me of how something that I said or done, encouraged them greatly. This is often welcome and necessary for any Leader to continue on. I understand that I may not be able to reach the masses. I need to know that I'm reaching somebody, because that makes the journey of ministering worth the while.

I feel motivated when I see families come back together. I love it when faith takes root in the heart of Believers and they begin to grow and prosper. When the effects of faith in the word begin to manifest itself and miracles take place. I've had the privilege of seeing families come back together. Those that were on the verge of divorce would find themselves reconnecting in church. I've seen children who were headed in the wrong direction, make a turn for better. I've experience faith move people from bad habits and addictions to total deliverance.

For me, the confirmation that I've been called to do this comes when I see the change in others. When someone walks up to me and says, "Pastor McGowan, if it wasn't for you, I wouldn't be married." I heard one lady say, "Pastor McGowan, if it wasn't for you, we wouldn't have a family." This couple could not have kids and wanted some badly. They decided to take part of a teaching called 'believing God for your miracle.' They happened to come in during that time, and I just began to minister how God desire to do for us what man sees as impossible.

Just because the doctor, attorney, counselor, or whoever tells you they don't see a way, doesn't necessarily mean it is over. For what is impossible with man is possible with God. According to your faith; be it unto you. Whereas the man said no, God said yes.

There was something in my voice that resurrected their faith. I believe the Word is powerful when spoken by those who truly believe it themselves. It's hard to convince others when you have not been convinced. I know the Word works and I know the power of prayer. These are the two things that have been consistent in my life since I was a small child. I believe I've turned into my mother. Sitting in the dew of the morning, praying for a family that is sound asleep.

My philosophy is: if I can help one somebody as I travel along, then my living is not in vain. I believe I have accomplished that for at least one somebody.

We have many divorced people in church. I've had some to say, "Pastor McGowan, if I had known you, I might still be married. I didn't have anybody to talk to me the way you talk to me. I didn't have anybody to be real." I hear this all the time. I respond, "Well, this is all I've got, me. What you see is what you get." I think even in pastoring, God has called me to pastor from a place of, being naked and not ashamed. I do my best. I pastor a generation of people who don't want you just to preach to them, they want a glimpse inside your life. I have no problem with that because if they know I have problems, if they know I have struggles, it makes them feel like they can make it. But if I stand over them and pretend I don't have any issues, then they can't identify with me. Most will just walk away from church.

I pastor from a place that I call nakedness. Nakedness means, I have to come in and admit that I hurt, I'm tired, I'm frustrated and I don't want to be here. I have to come in and just be real. I don't live on top of a mountain. I spend days, weeks and months in the valley. And I know they appreciate it. I had to come in and be frank about my own marriage and solicit their prayers. "I broke up with him, but I'm not going anywhere" I tell them. We break up in the house, but nobody's leaving, nobody's moving, nobody's going anywhere. We do have our moments, just like everybody else. Most people, especially married couples, have somehow convinced themselves that they are the only ones struggling in marriage, finances, with children, and careers, but that's just not true. Life is happening to all of us. None of us is exempt from life. Be it sickness, be it with children, be it with finances, we all have seasons we have to walk through. Those are the seasons when we really have to trust in God. I have to be that example for them. I can't give up. I can't bow, I can't break, and I can't bend. I have to remind myself of what He's already done in my life. And with passion and enthusiasm, I pull the praise report of God in my life.

CHAPTER 21

I remind myself, as I tell them my testimony of how God sent me home early from work. While living in Fort Meade, Maryland, I worked at the Exchange. I clocked out on Christmas Eve and came home. Little did I know that I had clocked out an hour earlier than I was scheduled to? We lived on the base, which made driving to and from work brief. I come home and rush upstairs to put on my get-ready-to-cook-clothes, sweats. It is Christmas Eve and I have lots of cooking to do. Breon had a cold and we had her on the couch because we were babying her. Evan was a very active two-year-old at the time. I take carrots from refrigerator and walk over to the sink. I wash them and begin shredding.

Just then, I hear my husband screaming in the front room. Evan had stopped breathing. Evan had gone and lay on top of his sister, who was lying on the couch. Breon says, "Daddy, something is wrong with Evan." So Bernard is looking at Evan and sees he has stopped breathing and is blackening around his eyes and ears because he's not getting any oxygen. My husband is a big guy—he's six-foot-two, 260 pounds—and he picks this baby up and is shaking him because he's not breathing. Every time he shakes him, he's yelling, "Monica! Monica!"

I come out of the kitchen with a carrot in my hand and a shredder, and Bernard is shaking this baby. I drop the stuff and grab my baby, and the Holy Spirit, once again, tells me what to do, *He's not breathing.*

Breathe into him. I've never done CPR, but I've seen it done, so I swept his mouth because he wasn't breathing. I had rolled back his head and knew he wasn't breathing. His ears had blackened, and he wasn't getting oxygen, so I swept his mouth to make sure nothing was stuck in there, and I began to breathe in him. Now, my husband and another soldier were there watching football, and they couldn't even dial 911. When it's your child that is in trouble, you may not respond with a level head. My husband lost it. This man had help save lives but, when it came to his child, he totally lost it. I'm breathing into Evan, and Bernard can't even dial 911. He and another sergeant, TC, they couldn't dial 911, so I have to try to save this child and dial 911 at the same time. "Hand me the phone!" I say, and I dial 911. The operator comes on.

"I have a two-year-old, and he's not breathing," I say. "I don't know what's wrong with him, but he's not breathing 'Help!'"

I'm hollering for help. We're in Maryland, it's snowing outside, and I'm sitting in the front door with the door wide open because I'm feeling, for some crazy reason, like I need to get Evan outside in the air. I don't know what that was about, but I'm sitting in my front door, I'm breathing into Evan, I've got his head tilted, and I'm talking to 911, saying, "He's not breathing, he's not breathing." At the same time, I'm breathing into Evan, but he was so little, and his stomach was so sunken in, I didn't want to mash his little ribs. You know how you're supposed to pump them? Well, not with a small child. I had to use just four fingers to press on his small chest.

Evan begins to throw up. The 911 operator says, "That's a good thing, that's a good thing!" I turn him to his side to keep him from choking. Now, my neighbor was a Christian, and he and I didn't talk all the time, but Breon and his little boy played together outside. I would see them going to church, and they would see us going to church. This man literally comes outside and stands on the corner of his yard and lifts his hand in the air and begins to pray. By the time I see him standing there,

I see the ambulance coming down Baker Street, and Evan and I get into the ambulance. We're on base, so the hospital is a short ride.

We found out that at the age of two, Evan is epileptic. Evan had what's known as a febrile seizure. These seizures just come on without notice. Within minutes the temperature rises and the child goes into seizure. There are no warning signs to look for! We would just have to pay close attention to him. On Christmas Eve we find out that our son is epileptic. My story reminds me of Shunammite's son. I had prayed and ask God for this child. What in the world is going on?

CHAPTER 22

When Evan had that seizure, once again I left a job. I started a home daycare. The base would qualify me to do home daycare. I began to care for children in my home. I knew how I would want my child cared for and that is how I would care for the other children. I could not trust anyone to watch Evan like he needed. There were no indication that a seizure was coming; they just happen. I felt like that level of responsibility had to come from his mom. If God was going to take him, it was going to be on my watch. I left my job, and I went through the 4 week process of getting state certified. Once my home was declared safe; I took on three other kids. I enjoyed them as much as I enjoyed my own children.

Evan is healthy now, and preparing for college. He is CNA certified in the state of Georgia, and manages to maintain a 3.4 GPA. He did the breathing treatments until age four or five. He is free of epileptic seizures and breathing problems. God delivered him from his childhood diseases.

In first grade, we were told he was ADHD. It wouldn't be until second grade that I'm convinced. He could not sit still and pay attention, so we started a regiment of Concerta and Ritalin. I took the medicines with him the first month because I needed to know the effects. I hated it and begin praying for deliverance. It kept us up at night and it gave us frequent headaches. I was able weaned him off of the medication with the Lord's help. Around seventh or eighth grade he was completely off. I refused to allow him to become a statistic and be treated differently than other children. He began to notice that his classes were smaller as well as what the other classes were working on. This bothered him and often he came home depressed. While playing football and other after school activities, the other kids begin to tease him about being in Special Education. Of course if it affects my child, it affected me. I took my child back to the Lord 'cause that is where I got him from.

I advise my kids, now that there are grown; if they're going to drink, to stay where they are at. I was there age once! They have both called and said, "Mom, I'm not coming home." I say, "All right, I'll see you tomorrow." I'd rather have them call and tell me there're drunk and not coming home or to come and get them, rather than have the police to call and tell me they've wrapped their car around a tree. Not everybody will agree but, these are my children. I will walk away from the church before I turn my back on my child. I will never forget to remember; I haven't always been who I am today. I don't want them to make dumb decisions and taking chances like I once did. I thank God all the time for taking the wheel of my car and driving me home safely.

Chapter 23

My advice on raising children is to allow them to become who they are. Remember that your kids are not you, and you are not your parents. We must allow them make mistakes. Understand that their mistakes are not final and do not define who they are. When you look at it, the Bible says we are all created in His imagine, fearfully and wonderfully made. We're all unique individuals. In one of my sermons, it dawned on me that I did not trust God with my children. Oh it's easy to tell others what the Word say but, preachers must take heed also. The Bible says to bring them up in the way they should go, and when they are older, it won't depart from them. I came to a place in the last few years, where I threw up my hands. "Lord, I've done my part and the rest is up to you." I brought them up in the church, I've taught them your laws and statues, and now I leave them in your hands. I understand they're going to make decisions that will cause me to shake my head. I too made decisions that my parent strongly disapproved. My mother couldn't believe she birth a few of us because of the paths we would journey.

Our children have to be given room for mistakes. We've all made mistakes but, we made it. He is the same God yesterday, today and forever more. If He brought me out, then I have to trust that He will bring my children through also. We would love to shield them from all the temptations, snares and trials of life but, we cannot. Every mistake

I've made has now turned into a testimony. It's my struggles not my successes that brings the glory. The best advice usually comes from those who been there and done that. Those who can identify with the pain, addiction, affliction, condition or shame that comes from making wrong choices. Our witness becomes believable when we can show others our scars. Our children are the next generation that God will use to evangelize this gospel. If we try to prevent them from going into the wilderness, they'll never know the power of God nor will they recognize the tricks of the enemy. We get years to train them how to call on the name that is above every name. That name is Jesus.

CHAPTER 24

I've been jotting down pages in notebooks since '87, shortly after my abduction. Writing became therapy for me. After my abduction, I went on a rollercoaster ride. Sometimes you're up, sometimes you're down. I had to fight depression; I had to fight that dark place, so I began to journal during different seasons of my life. A song on the radio, or something on television would trigger something inside of me and I would find myself crying. I would just start writing. I wrote about how I felt, about what I was doing when the tears came, how ugly rape was and NOONE talked about it. There were parts of the abduction that I had not dealt with but, I had no one to talk too. I felt like I was the only woman in the whole world who had been raped. On the other hand I felt like I couldn't talk about it because it was too personal. I still cringe when writing about this particular part of my journey.

Earlier in the year, around March or April, my husband, who retired from the military, went back over to Afghanistan as a contractor. This means that I will have lots of time to myself. My kids are grown and have their own lives. In April of this year, on a Sunday afternoon after church, I came home and redressed, and headed to the beach. I love being by the water. It's so relaxing and it soothes my inner being. I can think clearly when I'm there near the water. I'm there on the beach when an old white gentlemen approach me. Whether he was human or an angel, I'm not really sure, even now, a year later. But he had a beautiful set of eyes. Eyes so blue you could swim in them. He just began to talk to me.

"Have you told your story?" he asked.

"Excuse me, sir?"

"Have you written the story?" he asked again.

"No, I haven't written my story," I replied.

"Well," he said, "you need to tell your story. They're waiting to hear your story."

"What are you talking about?" I asked.

"Didn't God perform a miracle in your life?"

Immediately, I knew what he was talking about. I was overwhelmed at the fact that I'm talking to a stranger about something that took place in my life over twenty years ago. I stood starring into his eyes and begin to tremble all over. Yet, I felt a sense of peace. I felt like we were old friends who haven't seen each other in a long time. The same feeling I had in the ambulance with the paramedic. A stranger wouldn't have this kind of information, so he had to know me. We both smiled as he walked off and then completely out of sight. I sat on the beach, looking in the direction he had gone, before standing to my feet. I walked in the direction that he had gone, and then returned back in my car. I thought to myself, *maybe this is where my journey has taken me now. Maybe I need to take some time and write my story. What if my story can help someone? What if the thing that I went through wasn't about me? What if it was intended to bring healing to others who may have gone through similar situations? I didn't have anyone to talk too and I wouldn't wish that on anybody. Is it fair for me to know what I know and not care about others? A million questions ran through my mind as I sat there. I placed my face in my hands and begin to weep. My story is too ugly to share it will only embarrass me and my family. How can I share my life with the world, they will only judge me? I look toward the great blue ocean; "Lord, let your will be done in me" I murmured before starting the car.*

I stopped by the store and got a couple of writing tablets as I drove toward home. I began to write. I begin to write like a man freed from bondage runs for his life. I felt as if the words spoken at the beach had been sent to release me. I began to write around April, and didn't stop until I felt the need to get professional help. I decided I would go ahead, although I had never considered writing a book or anything, and see if it was possible. Most of my writings were just me giving myself therapy, trying to stay balanced. I wrote in order to stay alive. If the words found in my writings has caused me to continue living then I have no choice but, to offer the medicine found in its content, to others who suffer from the same illness. It would be selfish to the cure for a major disease and not share it. Maybe it won't cure everyone but, if one could find healing, that would be satisfaction enough.

As I continue to write and share my life, my faith, my journey on blank pages, I prayed that healing come to those, who may come after me and find my written words of inspiration. Please know that God is not through with me yet. I'm a work in progress. As long as there is pen and paper, I know, I will be alright.

CHAPTER 25

I had a moment of deliverance a few years ago. I had convinced myself that I was alright when God shined a light in one of my dark places. I'd gotten an invitation to go riding on a four-wheeler one Sunday after church. The ministry consists of whites, blacks and whosoever will type people. Well the couple that invited me just happens to be white. The family owns acres of land and enjoys the privacy of riding their ATVs. They own six in different sizes, colors and speeds.

Brother Ron said, "Pastor, get on one, we're going to go through the woods."

I get on, but I can't get the thing to go. So Bro. Ron says, "Hop on with me."

I hop on the back, and we take off. The family owns many acres of land with lakes and ponds. I'm holding on for dear life as we drives into the woods. OMG! My body just began to shake. It was fun at first, hopping over lakes, and speeding down paths. But I look and we're in the mist of nowhere and all alone. I'm shaking because it was exactly like the place my attacker had taken me. He's brought me here to kill me. He knew the exact location so that there would be no witnesses and no one could hear me scream. If I jump off and run, I wouldn't know which direction to go or how to make it back to the main house. He has no idea of what I had been through, and I had convinced myself that I was alright. I'm squeezing him like crazy, and my body is shaking so he comes to a complete stop and looks at me.

"Are you okay?" he asks, but I can't even answer him. I am totally freaked out.

"I'll get you back," he says. "I'll get you back."

Poor thing, he didn't know what to do, but he takes me back to where everyone else is. He gets off, and he's looking at me like he's done something wrong. I close my eyes and calm myself. I knew I had to explain what just happen. I realized there was a place I had somehow fortified in my heart, so that I would never be hurt again by a white man. Being alone in the woods with a white man, in the mist of nowhere, brought back the horror of the night of my abduction.

I called them over to my house a few days later to share my testimony about what I had gone through. Of course, they had no idea. In the three years that they had been with me it was never brought up. I'm often question about my scars but, they hadn't inquired and I didn't share it. But, after the incident at their ranch, I felt it necessary. I had to share with them because they were wonderful people and I didn't want any ill feelings. I didn't want them to think I was crazy or that they had done something wrong. The truth was I was afraid of being alone with a white man. I still harbored fear and I had to deal with them in order to move forward. I believe God had sent him, to help deliver me. He had shined his light in the crack where fear resided for years. If I was going to welcome all to the ministry, then my fear of white men had to be resolved. I didn't realize that I had become prejudice and had built up resentment. My being attacked by one white man had caused me to hate all white men. Just because we put things in the back of mind to never discuss again, is not deliverance. I had to confess in order to be delivered. If I was anywhere by myself and there were white men in my perimeter, I wouldn't even exit my car. If I was at an ATM and the vehicle behind me had a white male, I would drive off. I would drive to another location. The scars on my physical body had been cared for by the many doctors that I have seen. The scars to my mental and emotions had been cared for by Psychologist. The scars to my heart had been cared for by my husband and children. But, where does one go when the soul is wounded. The scars that are hidden need as much attention as those that are visible. They should be given the same consideration as the obvious scars which are given extra-special care.

It wasn't hard to share my story; it was just something I hadn't done in a while. Now when I began the ministry, I would get calls to come and share my testimony. In sharing my story, I didn't have to go into great details. I'd been called to women's conferences to minister to women hurting women. Those who had been molested, raped, physically abused, sexually abused would seek me out after service. I would stay for hours trying to encourage them not to remain the victim. If God brought us out, surely he has a plan for our lives. I loved sharing my story to help others. But, it had been years since I'd even had to talk about it. I don't just talk about it, unless someone is dealing with a situation and my story will help.

I guess when you put it on the back burner, you forget it's there, but yet, it's still there. It didn't feel good to tell them, because of why I have to tell them. I was traumatize to say the least and needed to explain. I was totally embarrassed at my behavior. This will never happen to me again because I will deal with it now. Anything brought into the light, loses its power. This thing will not hold me bondage any longer. I will not be a silent victim to fear.

Sister Pam begins to weep. She is the sweet, quiet wife of Ron. In sharing my story, it brought light to her dark childhood secrets. I stop talking as she became liberated to share her own personal story of abuse. She began to share what had happened with her as a little girl. She had been abused by an uncle. Talking about the abuse wasn't allowed and therefore she was in need of healing. To be abuse then not be allowed to talk about it is the same as being cut and not being allowed to bleed. We all ended up holding hands and praying, one for another. They are very familiar with a phrase I use all the time: life is happening to all of us; none of us are exempt from life. We see each other, but we don't really know each other. It's impossible to really know each other if we only spend three or four hours together within our church walls. I believe you have to walk with people for a season, to really get to know them. I believe that experience of them inviting me out to the farm to ATV was ordained by God to bring deliverance not only to me but, also to Sister Pam. The steps of the righteous are ordered by the Lord.

When you stand to minister to others, you've got to be free. You don't get to pick and choose how or where. The word is sharper than any two-edge sword. The family continued with me after this event. They would have family to come and connect with the ministry because of the maturity and growth in their life. When someone else can see the change for the better taking place in us, then they will be compelled to come. If what we are doing is not causing change in our lives, we will never be able to convince others. We must be first partakers of the word of God. Let it first be effective in us. When the fruit of the Word bring forth fruit in my life, those around will see and believe. The changes that took place in Brother Ron and Sister Pam's lives demanded the attention of all who knew them. They now have an aunt that visit. She is an older woman with some health issues but, when she's feeling up to it, she worships with us. She always gives the best hugs. I'm her black angel!

I talk to real people, from a real place and always will. I let them know that I don't live every day on top of the mountain. Some days, I'm down in the valley. My desire is that they always leave with something that will help them in their day to day lives. I share with the ladies, how I struggled with depression. I share how I begin to study the signs that came along with depression. Once I recognize the signs then I figured out how to better it. When I feel myself going into that dark place, how I pick up my bible and begin to read scriptures out loud. The bible says that faith comes by hearing. So I need to hear in order to be strengthened. I would then pick up the phone and make a call. I call someone who may not have to service. I call and encourage others while at the same time I'm encouraging myself. There is something simply amazing about encouraging others that brings encouragement. When I don't want the window shades open, don't want to be bothered with people, and don't want to get out of bed. I find the simplest task impossible to do. I would isolate myself from the rest of the world. We will never be free if we continue to deny that we have a problem. Denial is a weapon that the enemy has and will continue to use against all of us.

CHAPTER 26

Prayer is the key, but it's faith that opens doors. We must have faith on this journey. It's our faith that brings the victory. My mother had eleven children and all eleven of us consider her to be, a great woman of faith. Her testimony during the time I was being abducted will inspire many. I can share all of this now, although I didn't know it then.

During the time of my abduction, my mom said the spirit of God woke her on that very night. She said the Holy Spirit began to minister to her to pray and intercede for her children because one of her children was in trouble. My mom shared that she thought it was one of her sons. She never thought that one of her daughters was in trouble. It really didn't matter; my mom prayed from midnight to six in the morning. She said she could not sleep! She just got up and began to walk the floor and began to pray. She began to bombard heaven: *Lord, watch over my children. Save them and place your shield of protection around them.* It was right after mid-night that I was abducted and about six the next morning they found me. It was shortly after she'd prayed that the call came from Carolina. As a Believer her story keeps me on my face concerning my own children. It amazes me to know that while I'm fighting for my very life; my mother was interceding in prayer on my behalf. The prayers of the righteous availeth much.

My mother and father in Georgia, and I'm in Asheville, North Carolina.

They got the call that something had happened and they needed to hurry and get up there. I don't know if the police called or my sister. The sister that I was living with couldn't handle it at all. From what I was told, she passed out, and she was no help to anybody. She felt responsible and like Mom and Daddy was going to kill her. They didn't want me to leave in the first place. They knew there were things in a big city that I was naïve too. The doctors didn't know if I was going to live; all they knew was that I was messed up and had to go into surgery.

My parents along with other family members rushed to Asheville. My mother would later share with me her decision for the doctor to administer abortion medicines. Once at the hospital she would receive further details of what had happened to include rape. In hearing the details of the trauma I had suffer, she would have to make for me a decision that I was in no way capable of making for myself. Time was of the essence and she was the only person I'd want making such decisions for me. The medication is given without a pregnancy test. I wasn't on any type birth control and had been rape, so the possibility of being impregnated by my abductor was valid. I will be forever grateful for this decision.

My mother didn't tell me until we came home and after everything was settled in Carolina. We had to go through hearings for my abductor to be sentenced. My mother was with me throughout this whole process. She didn't agree on my leaving home and coming to the city but, she never mention it and took her place by my side. After we came home, I began to relax, and we would sit and talk. I would better understand after each conversation with mom and other members of my family. Evidently there were moments and periods of this event that I didn't remember. I would need to talk with each and everyone involved to bring all the pieces together. In order to have it all make some kind of sense, I would need to talk and continue to talk with all of them concerning what happen.

After they stitched me all back up, they asked if I was on birth control, and I guess my sister and my niece said no, I didn't take birth control. The statement was that there was a possibility that I could be pregnant, and that they had some type of medicine, a pill, that would ensure that if there had been a pregnancy, there wouldn't be a pregnancy anymore. My mom and my big sister made the decision just to give me the pill. They agreed that I wouldn't be able to handle a child coming out of such trauma. The things I found out about later were very interesting. We laugh about my mom being slow getting pack and daddy talking about leaving her. My brothers and sisters had to put their money together for gas and drive whoever had the best car. We laugh about how they plan to kill the man that had hurt me. Which one of them would get the first punch if they got to see him? My brothers were going take turns punching and kicking him in the head. I now realize how much they love me. They were really to go to jail!

CHAPTER 27

As a Christian woman, I knew I had to forgive him. I will never forget what happen but, I have forgiven my abductor and I did it years ago. If I hadn't released him then I would remain his victim and I refuse to give him any power over me. I have no bitterness, I have no hatred, nor do I have harsh words. I've ponder going to visit him in prison. I would love to look him in his face and say, "I forgive you." As a Pastor I would offer the gift of salvation and prayer. That's something I'm throwing around now. When we visit Asheville, that's something we are going to inquire about.

We were able to pull him up online. There is a site where you can do inmate inquiries. There he was—his picture, his crime, everything. As I read the charges, I thought, *oh my God, that's me.* The knife, the rape, the murder, the kidnapping, the assault with a deadly weapon—all of those crimes, they were against me. Someone had told me awhile back that you could pull up inmates online with their pictures. You know me—Ms. CSI! I kept looking until I found it. I remember when I found him and his picture came up, I grabbed my mouth going, *oh my God, that's him. That is him! A fellow minister had to console me. I never expected my reactions to be what they were.*

CHAPTER 28

I'm hoping that women who have had similar tragedies in their lives will read my book. I'm hoping that husbands and sons will read it in order to help them understand the wife, the mother, the daughter, the sister or the aunties in their lives. I'm hoping that pastors will read it. I'm hoping that everyone will read it, because it's going to help someone that your life is attached to. If not you, we all know somebody.

I remember doing a women's conference down in Florida, and after the service was over, these little old ladies came up to me. One of them said to me, "Thank you so much," and she said her uncle had disturbed her. She didn't say rape, she didn't say molest, she said disturbed. She said, "My uncle disturbed me when I was a little girl." I think as women, we try to hide the ugly parts in our past. I have a saying that anything brought into the light loses its' power. Anything you hide, you can't get over. You have to bring it into the light so it no longer has power over you. As long as we keep it locked in, it can control us.

It's kind of like Brother Ron and I. As long as I had this thing in the dark place, I wasn't really dealing with it. I never had to really confront the fact that I had built up a prejudice against white men. We can hid things so well that we too will begin to deceive ourselves into thinking we're ok when we're not. God will allow events to take place in our lives to shine light on the darkness. It's really up to us how we react when we're uncovered. I can deal with the truth and be delivered, or I can deny it and stay in bondage to it. I chose to be free!

God uses people; I believe everybody attached to our life has a purpose in it. Some are there for reasons, some are there for seasons, but every person in your life has some significance. We have to value these relationships and really investigate and invest into them. We need to look and see what it is that each person brings to the table. We must ask *why you are in my life. What is your significance?*

I believe life is a journey. It's a book, and every year we're writing chapters, and in each chapter, you have different characters. In this particular chapter that I'm walking now, I've got different characters. In the next chapter, some of the characters remain, some exit, and then you've got new characters. That's how life is. We go in and out of seasons, and in and out of our chapters. God has to send people in and out of our lives to make us who He's called us to be. Another thing I've come to conclude is that; He takes all of the good, the bad, and the ugly; to make us. The person we are today is not the person we're going to be ten years from now. We're all going to be somebody different; we're evolving. Life is a journey.

I believe my two children will read this book. I can't be certain but, I pray that they will. They will automatically become eye witnesses to many of the events. I think they would read it to see where and how I grew up. As parents, we often tell our children bits and pieces of our upbringing. We offer them a window into how things were while we were growing up. The clothes we wore and the hair styles. How much different we are from our own parents. Our children currently enjoy pleasures that were not available to us growing up in rural Georgia. It wasn't until we were adults that we realize we were just like every other family.

The impact I would like my book to make on readers is that you can go through a horrible situation and still come out with victory. That is really the totality of it. I don't want them to think that because something bad happened, you've got to stay there. You don't have to be the victim forever. A lot of people, once they're victimized, remain victims for the rest of their life. My psychiatrist made the statement that I would be unable to have a normal life. The abduction had given me a fear of men; so getting married and having children was out of the picture. Just for the record, I've been married twenty-four years with two children and two godsons. Now if this is not normal, then I'm clueless as to what normal really means.

If you've got somebody constantly feeding you with negative thoughts or if you're feeding negativity to yourself, then you need to make a change. Change what you're hearing and change what you're saying. The things that we constantly say are the things that we are seeing manifest on our journey. Life and death is in the power of the tongue. We must understand and speak in a positive voice. What we tell ourselves is what we have a tendency to believe and what we believe we will eventually speak. Faith comes by hearing and hearing by what's being spoken; in faith; in our ears. If we don't like what we are seeing in our lives then we must begin to change what is being planted. Words are seeds in the garden of life. You will never see in your garden, what hasn't been planted, either by you or someone you trust. It's time to take inventory of what's being produced in your life. If it doesn't bear good fruit, it must be uprooted and destroyed immediately. We must speak those things that bring life.

CHAPTER 29

Please understand; the Lord sent someone to love me like He loves me. I needed a man who would love me in spite of myself. My husband fell in love with me when I didn't love myself, when I didn't think myself to be attractive. I went through a phase after being abducted that I didn't want to be attractive. I did everything possible to fade into the background. I feared attracting the wrong type of attention from the wrong type of man and did my best to go unnoticed. The same hair that had been curled and styled daily was now pulled back into a ponytail. The expensive make up that I had been professionally trained to apply went into the trash. I didn't want to do anything that would attract a man of any color to me. I did not want anyone looking at me! Being attractive is what drew my abductor and I didn't want to be a future target. Of course at eighteen and nineteen years old, you think you're the cutest girl alive. We live for lip gloss and lipstick, eyeliner and eye shadow because it enhanced our youthful radiance. My husband would have to find a wife without these things. He would have to be able to look pass the outward appearance and find something attractive on the inside. He would have to be someone special with x-ray vision. We have a tendency to dress outwardly according to how we feel inwardly. I now believe that God hid me deep into depression because He knew, the only way for a man to convince me to come out, was after I first allowed him to come in.

Chapter 30

He will never leave nor forsake us. There are so many instances on my journey that I became lost and wandered in darkness. I had a five-speed, and I Remember one morning, I drove myself home. I had put the car in neutral but, left it running. One of my brothers was getting up going to work, and he knocked on the window and said, "Turn the car off, stupid!" I remember he woke me up. Somehow I made it home, into my mom's yard, safely, but how I got there, I don't know. Once again, the hand of the Lord was covering me. I left the car running and was in the car asleep, passed-out drunk, with the windows up. When my brother knocked on the window, I remember thinking to myself, *you have a problem,* but I didn't have the strength to stop.

For my mom, she was being the best mom she could be, but for me, I needed something else, and I didn't know what it was. I knew she was praying but, I had this void. My husband and I often say that God used the both of us to save each other's life. I was his life raft and he was mine. I truly believe that if he had not come along when he did, there's no telling where I would be, what I would be doing, or who I would be as a person. I could have been dead or have killed someone. I could be in prison for manslaughter or confined to a wheelchair. We just don't know! Our journey takes us places that are embarrassing until, we cross paths of those who need to hear our story. Then that which was embarrassing becomes a testimony to the help others to live.

For me, I had to get down the road to really look back and see the hand of God on my life. When you're in it, you can't always see what He's doing. Sometimes you have to go through it and get the victory before you testify. Everybody doesn't make it out of everything. Some of the things I came out of, I know there are those who did not. When you look back, in the corridors of your mind, you become a vital witness. When you can confess, "If it had not been for the Lord, who was on my side" I would have been taken out of here. It's such an eye opener when you can recognize the tender mercy of God being extended to all. There will never be a Halloween that I fail to give thanks for my very life.

My husband and I have two grown children. I have experience miraculous things all of my life. From my childhood to the very present, miracles are taking place. I have turned somewhat into my mom, and now I've got children that are experiencing His power. It would be a travesty to introduce our children to everything in this world and fail to introduce them to the one that created it. My daughter will be lost knowing what a bad outfit is and not know how to call on the name of Jesus. We introduce our children to education, money, fame and all sort of things but, if we fail to introduce them to the creator, we've failed them tremendously.

CHAPTER 31

One thing that I hope will be unique about this book is the fact that I write from the office of a Pastor. As an ordained minister, I've like reading personal growth help books. Right now, I'm reading Dr. Wayne Dyer's *believe it then you'll see it,* and *Think and Grow Rich by Napoleon Hill.* I love reading books that inspire. Once I find that author, I will often time become a faithful follower. My husband and I owned a Christian bookstore that we sold a few years ago, and I have never seen a book that allows others a view into the life faith based leadership. Most faith leaders give the false impression that their life has somehow been exempt for everyday events and they've never done any wrong.

I think as leaders in the body of Christ, when we can stand and tell our stories, it will liberate others. The body of Christ will rise up and become the powerhouse it was originally intended to be. As long as we continue to hide and wear mask, then those that we lead will continue to do the same. We all have a story to tell. The Bible says we are one body in Christ, each joint supplying. I believe when we uncover the truths in our lives and experiences, others can look and say, *okay, they did it; maybe I also stand a chance of making it.* I have to share my life with others because I refuse to have them think that I live on top of a mountain. The thing that drove me crazy was thinking no one in the world had been rape or husband had been unfaithful. We have the answers to the questions that the world is asking if we will unmask and tell them how we got through our own experiences.

My experience really is a big part of my ministry. I believe that most ministries that start from the ground up, like OEW, must spin of a miracle. You have to know without a shadow of a doubt that there is a powerful being beyond human ability that exists, and we have access to Him is vital. How can we otherwise confirm that higher power except we've have a personal encounter. It is a vital part of my ministry and that will be successful.

If I can get one somebody to give me feedback and say that this book has helped them, then it's a success. My old pastor singed a song: "If I can help one somebody as I travel, than my living is not in vain." If I can help just one somebody, this book is not in vain. If I can help one somebody see that they are traveling wrong or that they don't have to stay in depression or bondage, then it's a success. I'm not trying to reach the masses but, thank God if I do. I'm trying to reach that one person who thinks that life is over. I need you to know that all things work together for the good of them that love the Lord; to them that are called according to His purpose.

CHAPTER 32

The hardest part of my abduction—something I am still working on within myself—is the rape part. As I write my story, I come to a place during the rape, where I just have to drop my pen and weep. I've never been able to verbalize this part of my testimony. I try to talk about it but, I find a way out with anyone who has not been through it themselves. I'm still trying to figure out why it is so hard to say what happened in the backseat of that car. I believe that sex is intimate and should only be shared between those in agreement with each other. That part I will struggle with until someone brings understanding that is reasonable to me. My rape will play a role in how I deal with the extramarital affair of my own husband, years later. But, I'm determined to get up and face each day with a smile. I know I need to find my feet in that particular area and actually find words that will help others. I just briefly mention the forced oral sex and getting out of the car. I don't know if it's a block in my mind, or that I just don't want to deal with it verbally, per se, but that's the only part of it for which I haven't come to a place of peace. How do you put into words what happened? I just can't find the words or I don't know the words. I don't want it to be too graphic, but at the same time, I believe that when I say he did everything sexually to me that he wanted to do, that should cover it. Sex is still the most intimate part of being human. It should be considered sacred by anyone who has morale values.

Chapter 33

My father passed in 2002. My father was a hard worker, but he also was a bitter, angry man. I remember he worked very hard. As a little girl, I loved my daddy so, but when he would come home it was like all hell would break loose. When we would hear his truck pull up, it was like everybody would freeze. I'm the baby of eleven kids, and I understood as I got older that by the time I came along, he was much better. They had told me he had really calmed down. He would come home and just argue; he would just fuss about anything. Anything was a problem. I would run and jump on his leg because I was so happy that Daddy was home, and he would carry me back to his bedroom door. I would get off and jump on his back. It seemed like, in my recollection, that I was the only one that loved him in the house, or I was the only one that could show acts of love, because everybody else would freeze up.

My daddy used to argue all the time. He was a cussing man. He used to cuss; he would say what he wanted to say, and kids say what their parents say. So my dad would tell my mom to shut the hell up, and when I was about five or six, and he would get to fussing, I would sit in his lap and tell him to shut the hell up. Whatever I heard him say, I begin to start saying. One day, I slapped him and told him to shut the hell up. He looked at my mom and said, "This one ain't even mine." My mother said to him, "Oh yeah, that one is definitely yours."

It's like I had this love-hate thing for him. On the Fourth of July, we always went to the beach, and I remember so clearly that everybody would be in the water except for me. I would be standing holding my daddy's leg. I vividly remember one beach day in particular. "Stank," he said, because that was my nickname, "you see that boat out there?"

I looked way out on the horizon, and this boat was so far out that it appeared to be about the size of an ant.

My daddy said, "Go get in the water," but I wouldn't go.

"You see that boat out there?" he said. "That's how far I'll come to get you. Now, c'mon, go get in the water."

I remember letting go of his leg and splashing in the water because I knew my daddy was there and I didn't have to be afraid.

He was a caring father; he was a protector. I was off-balance with him. I loved him, but I hated him. Then I realized I didn't hate him, I just didn't like the bitterness. He came up so hard, and he had to provide for a family. Back then, my parents didn't know about food stamps and government assistance. Everything we got, Daddy worked and paid for. I had to wait until Daddy got the money to get eyeglasses or to go to the dentist. We would go to the doctor in sets of two, and we would also visit the dentist in sets of two. We just had to wait. My daddy wasn't an educated man, but he knew how to work. I think he was bitter because there seemed to be never enough. He always had to provide for this large family, but we began to get older and leave the nest. I think he was angry because he had to work, even when he was sick, he went to work. When I got older, my mom was able to go get a job. Though he was a mean man, he took care of us, and he was a protector. He would give his life for one of his kids. He told us he went to work when he was seven or eight years old. He had to go out into the fields and work, so all he knew was to work. Daddy never got the chance to be a child but, then he realized how better his family was than most of those around them.

Before God took him home, I was able to tell him that I loved him and that I appreciate him working hard and giving us his all. He gave us his all. I remember thinking when we were younger that we were poor, but as I got older and grew up, I realized we were doing much better than a lot of people were. I would like to tell Daddy thank you. Thank you for your blood, sweat, and tears; thank you for all you gave. Thank you for your gift of sacrifice that we took for granted. I appreciate it. I really do; I appreciate it.

Dad gave us the best. He had a Montgomery Ward credit card, and we would go school shopping once a year. We would all go over to Montgomery Ward and JC Penney's, and Daddy would get us all back-to-school clothes, coats, and shoes. Then he would make payments on it, and he paid it off every year. Every year, he would do the same thing, and I appreciate all of that. We didn't appreciate it back then, but we appreciate it now. In tenth grade, I had the opportunity to visit one of my friend's houses, and when we got there, I found she didn't have a bathroom. They didn't have an inside bathroom, and I thought, *oh my goodness!* We were doing much better than a lot of people. I felt sorry after I got older because I thought we were the poorest of the poor, but we weren't. We were really blessed; we just didn't know we were blessed.

So, I appreciate Daddy for all that he gave. I wish he could know that I'm living my best life, and that he instilled in me what a man is supposed to do. He instilled in me what to look for in a man. I wish he were here to understand that I am writing a book, and that his name would be called in the book, and that he would be proud. I believe he is looking down now, and he's proud. Before he passed, the question was who would take care of my mom, Myrtle. He would say, "Who's going to take care of Myrtle?" I told my dad, "There are eleven of us. Mom will be fine. I'll take care of her." I would want him to know that Mom is well taken care of by her children.

CHAPTER 34

I believe I'm living to live again. This life is not final destination. I will see Him when this part of my journey concludes. I'm not sure what it will be like, but from what I've read and what I understand, every day is going to be Sunday. We're going to praise twenty-four seven. There won't be sickness, and there won't be pain. It's just going to be howdy, howdy, never goodbye. I can't even imagine, but in my mind, that's the best I can do. It's just going to be a glorious place, something that you can't imagine. Scripture says, "Eyes haven't seen, ears haven't heard. Neither has it entered into the heart of man what God has in store for those who love Him." When I look at that Scripture, I can't even imagine, because there is nothing here to be compared to it. It's going to be awesome.

I believe my dad is in that place now where he has no cares, no pain, and no sickness. When he got older, he began to get sick, and he struggled with high blood pressure, diabetes, and heart disease. I remember my mom giving him insulin shots in his thighs and sometimes in his butt. All of that is over; he doesn't have to deal with that anymore. We're going to a place where there are no broken hearts; no sickness, cancer, or heart disease; no high blood pressure, low blood pressure, or any blood at all. None of that stuff will exist, and it will just be wonderful. No one will have to worry about mortgage payments.

CHAPTER 35

I had a pastor I believe God used to minister to me and catapult me into the next level of my faith in Him. She was really a blessing. Her name was Pastor Betty. She got killed in a car accident while traveling to go preach, and I remember that I loved her with so much compassion. She was so loving and so kind. She was what I thought was the epitome of what we're supposed to be like as Christians. I loved her. I remember being so drawn to her, to the anointing that was on her life. I wanted her to not want for anything. It was so devastating for me, and many others, that God took her from us to be with Him.

About fifteen years ago, Pastor Betty ordained me into the ministry. She said, "God's going to use you, baby. You're going to take the Gospel all around the world." After she passed, I felt compelled and knew I had launch out in ministry. It would take two years but, the ministry got started. I had a dream where she was standing at the foot of my bed and smiling. She was smiling like a mother does at her baby in the crib, looking at him smiling, like he's her angel. I felt the warmth of her approval of what I was doing.

She had spoken over my husband and I saying, God was going to use us to take the ministry farther. My husband does what's called live streaming on Sundays, and our services are streamed live over the

Internet. Even while he's over in Afghanistan, he is able to watch the service and share it with others. He emails the message also to those on our email list. So I reflect on what she said, about God using us to take the ministry to other countries. The prophecy has come to pass.

CHAPTER 36

When I say that my father was mean, he was. I grew up in a house where my father was verbally abusive. Probably around seventh grade, I couldn't stand before a group of my peers and read publicly. I would begin to shake so because of the verbal abuse I was getting at home. I was in my first year of college when I realized that it was because of my father. We had to do a paper in school, and you had to read your paper in order to get the hundred percent. I remember turning my paper in, and my professor read it and wanted me to read it aloud to the class. Of course, I was not going to do that because I could not read verbally in front of my peers. She gave me a seventy-five, but she knew the paper was good and reading it would have guaranteed me 100%. I thought the paper was good, too, I just I could get by without reading it.

When my husband and I joined the ministry, Pastor Betty asked me to begin to read scriptures. Also, when she would go out, she would want to me to introduce her. I used to get sick because I had to do this. I couldn't eat, I couldn't sleep, and I'd have diarrhea and stomach cramps leading up to that time when I had to do this. She used to say to me, "You speak so well. God's got you in training, baby, c'mon." I remember one time standing up to introduce her, and my knees were literally knocking. I don't know if the congregation understood what I said or not. Sweat was running down my legs, and I was literally sick. When I sat down, I thought, *okay, I'm glad that's over*. I did that for a long time, but I loved her so much that when she asked me to do something, I would do it despite the fear.

Joyce Meyer has a book called *Do It Afraid*, which I found in one of the Christian bookstores—we didn't have ours back then. I remember reading it over and over. It's like sometimes, you've got to do it afraid. I began to introduce Pastor Betty, and I got more comfortable doing it. Then, she would just ask me to teach a Bible study. I'm thinking, *I can't teach a Bible study*! But, she just began to train me and mold me in everything I thought I couldn't do. I believe the Lord helped her tweak that in me.

Now, I'm in place where I can talk for hours, and someone has to tell me to shut up. I came up from where I wouldn't even speak in front of a group of people because my father had verbally abused us at home. I didn't feel worthy. If your dad says you're nothing, then you can't be anything but nothing. That's why Pastor Betty is really a great presence, even now. Sometimes when I'm doing things in the ministry, I sense her approval. She stands as the voice of my heavenly father.

In the summer, we feed hundreds of people every day, and I feel her pat on the back saying that's right. She always told us a minister is really a servant. That's what the word minister means: to serve. If you aren't willing to serve, then you won't be effective in ministry. Anytime I'm out doing something, and I get tired and exhausted—and I do—I just remember her words, "God called you to serve. And if you don't want to serve, don't let anybody ordain you into the ministry." So we serve, and my kids serve. My son stands on the corner in the heat and waits for people in that area to come out and get those community lunches. I've taught my kids to serve. The Bible says, "The greatest among you, let them be your servants." I believe in the spirit of serving. I know my pastor would be proud. I think I channel her energy every now and then, especially when I get to a place of being overwhelmed and exhausted and fatigued. "Don't get weary in well doing; you'll reap if you faint not." I find strength in her words to keep going.

CHAPTER 37

One of the best days of my life is the day I knew I loved my husband. Let me try to explain. When I met my husband, I was not looking to be in love, I just wanted to date whoever I wanted to date. But, I remember the very day that I knew that I was in love with him. I remember I just began to weep because now he had the capability of hurting me, and I didn't want to be hurt.

That was one of the pinnacles in my life, just remembering that. I used to tell myself I would never fall in love. I wasn't going to have anything to do with it. I cried so much and couldn't explain why I was crying. Bernard called my mother to tell her that I was crying and he didn't know why. He promised that he'd done nothing wrong but, he didn't know what to do. He came home with a dozen roses and sub sandwich. He brought me everything I liked—he was trying to keep me from crying. I had to tell him I loved him; I had never said it before.

CHAPTER 38

In the next ten years, I see my husband and I being together. He is going to come home and stay for good. I see us building the ministry up. Part of my vision is to start an alcohol and drug program for teens and adults. I want to be able to help people in transition, be it a mom with kids coming from a divorce, or somebody coming out of jail, or families in transition, going from one place to another. I want to be able to be a great light, a beacon in the community that we live in.

We're both in our mid-forties, and I'm thinking the next ten or fifteen years will be dedicated to the ministry. Then, I'm thinking around sixty—if the Lord says the same —we're going to break away and take vacations around the world. There are many places we talk of visiting. The latter part of our journey together, we'd like it to just be me and him. My kids and my husband believe that they have had to share me with everybody in the community. As a minister, everybody knows you. You don't know them, but they become familiar with who you are. In my community, I'm unable to go into a store and just shop because I see somebody that knows me. I feel compel to stop on every aisle and acknowledge them. I'm looking forward to the next fifteen years; then we can retire and relax. Sit back and just enjoy each other and our grandkids.

My favorite place in the entire world is sitting in my house with my husband and our kids, just talking and laughing. That's my favorite place. You would think it would be Paris, but some of my fondest memories and happiest times are just the four of us. We don't have to be doing anything special, just being together is special enough and having each other's undivided attention.

My life is everything I could dream of. My faith keeps me focused on where I'm going and not where I am. My journey includes hurt, pain, suffering and rejection but, I wouldn't trade anything for my journey now.